CONFLICTS IN CRICKET

CONFLICTS IN CRICKET

JACK BAILEY

THE KINGSWOOD PRESS

The Kingswood Press
an imprint of Methuen London
Michelin House, 81 Fulham Road, London SW3 6RB

LONDON MELBOURNE AUCKLAND

Copyright © 1989 Jack Bailey
First published 1989

0 434 98166 4

Printed and bound in Great Britain by
Richard Clay Ltd, Bungay, Suffolk

To Julianne, Tim, Ali and Ros and to David, who lived through it with me and suffered accordingly.

CONTENTS

ACKNOWLEDGEMENTS

My thanks for help in writing this book must go first to my many friends in cricket who have always been an immense source of support. They come not only from within MCC, the greatest club, and throughout the country, but from all over the cricket-playing world, and thus are too numerous to men-. tion individually.

The production of this book owes more than I can say to Tony Pocock, a kindly, patient and wise editor, nursemaid and cajoler; and to Sally Clarke and Linda Parker whose help with the typescript was invaluable.

The photographs are published by kind permission of the *Daily Mirror* (no. 15), Patrick Eagar (nos. 1, 6, 7, 9, 10, 11, 12, 13 and 14), the *News of the World* (no. 8), R. L. Smerdon (no. 2), the Sport and General Press Agency (nos. 3 and 4) and *The Times* (no. 5).

PREFACE

I left Lord's, where I was Secretary of MCC and of the International Cricket Conference, at the end of January 1987 – the year of MCC's bicentenary. I had played a full part in the organization of events which were to celebrate 200 glorious years and had been looking forward to playing a part in them.

That I was on the outside looking in when the celebrations took place was down to me in the sense that I could have chosen to be a survivor rather than a victim of one of cricket's internal conflicts. It was simply that the price of survival had become too high for me, both as a person and as Secretary. For me, being Secretary of MCC was an honour. MCC is not just a cricket club, but an institution – a caring, influential institution – and had been part of my life since I first became a member in 1958. It was a great privilege to serve the Club, and through it to serve cricket, not only in England, but throughout the world. Now, alas, the scope of that job has been much diminished.

This book is about conflicts in cricket, but the happy times have always outweighed by far the difficult ones, and I owe that balance to everyone, almost without exception, who figures in this book.

1

PORTRAIT OF THE ARTIST AS A
YOUNGER MAN

CARL JUNG SAID that he was first aware of himself as an individual when he was eleven years old. Any comparison to be drawn between Carl Jung and me ends right here, but I suppose it was at a similar age, when I first went to Christ's Hospital, that I realized how much a part of my life cricket had become. Before then, in a spontaneous way, I had taken to all ball games and most of my spare time was taken up with playing in pick-up matches of soccer or cricket, many of them using a tennis ball on a concrete surface. At this stage I was largely self-taught. But, for all the technical errors this produced, I generally found that I was able to take wickets and score runs at least as well as my peers.

I was playing cricket when news of Len Hutton's record-breaking 364 against the Australians in 1938 came through. I had just finished a game of cricket when England's declaration of war against Germany was announced by Neville Chamberlain. I saw my first game of county cricket when my father took me to Canterbury where Kent were playing the Australians. I remember marvelling at the ease with which the great Frank Woolley plundered the Australian attack, especially the chinamen and googlies of 'Chuck' Fleetwood-Smith. I can still see the ball rattling around on top of one of the stands after one of Woolley's imperious blows, can still see the surprise and chagrin on the face of Bill Brown from Queensland, after he ran round the long-leg boundary, positioning himself for a high swirling catch on the run from Woolley's hook, only to tumble over the outstretched feet of some small boys who had strayed beyond the boundary ropes. The catch was spilled and so, very nearly, was the blood of one or two young spectators.

Christ's Hospital, during the middle years of the Second World War, presented those of us lucky enough to be there with an armful of golden opportunities, not all of which we were of an age to recognize. The teaching staff had been depleted by the calls of service, and many of those who left for the armed forces had been the most enthusiastic games players. But those sportsmen still on the staff rallied round, delighted in most cases with the opportunity to pass on their knowledge. Hector Buck, the master in charge of cricket and in his day a fine club wicket-keeper, recognized that in Len Bates, the school professional, there was a man to be nurtured and supported, rather than directed, and to his great credit gave him free rein. Between them, the school's cricket could not have been in better hands.

Len Bates was to become a considerable influence on my life and on that of many others. He had played for Warwickshire over a longish period between the wars as a fluent batsman who usually went in first wicket down, and his record over the years fell only just short of what was required to gain recognition for England. In 1933, when R. E. S. Wyatt was absent for the Glamorgan match, he captained Warwickshire and became the first professional to lead his county for twenty years. The esteem with which he must have been held in Warwickshire was unknown to those who came under his influence at school, for only rarely – so rarely for it to be a phenomenon if it happened – did he talk about his own life as a cricketer. What he did instil into people like Geoffrey Smith (who later played for Kent), Dennis Silk (now Warden of Radley College, following cricket for Cambridge University and Somerset), John Snow of Sussex and England, and myself, was a great love of the game in all its facets. If he ever raised his voice, I didn't hear it. Yet he had immense authority. What he taught us about cricket and, in so many ways, about life itself always turned out to be true. A selfless man, he tried to impart selflessness in us and usually, because he led by example, he was successful. He was a walking advertisement for all that was best in the professional cricketer between the wars. Having been born at Edgbaston, the son of the head groundsman, he looked after the Big Side pitches at Christ's Hospital with a tender, loving care which reflected his background.

Those were the days of George Geary at Charterhouse, of Tom Bowles at Eton, of Charlie Parker at Cranleigh. Days when rain, though unwanted, meant that if you played your cards right and the match was away from home, you might hear, say, Bates and Parker reminiscing about their days in the county game and – never maliciously – about some of the great household names, Hammond, Goddard, Wyatt *et al.*

I came early into Len Bates's orbit. My first summer at Christ's Hospital saw me appearing in the school Under-14 team. Len must have had his eye on me, because the following year found me in the Colts (Under-16) and the following year, at fourteen, I received a card to turn up for the initial 1st XI nets of the summer term: 2 o'clock was the time and, very unusually, I could hardly eat my lunch. Having changed at breakneck speed and after running the best part of a mile, I arrived at seven minutes before 2 o'clock, relieved to be well in time, but surprised that the nets were already in full swing. Boys were batting, boys were bowling. Len saw me and came over.

'Sorry I'm late,' I said. 'I thought nets began at 2 o'clock.'

'It's all right, you'll find that a lot of them are so keen they get here early,' he said.

It was nicely put and the nets almost became a second home. Playing in the school 1st XI at the age of fourteen, with and against people considerably older, taught me a great many things about human nature, as well as about cricket. The domestic heirarchical structure at school was such that fourteen-year-olds were not encouraged to be precocious and I was conscious that with the excitement and the glory came a need to be self-effacing, almost everywhere but on the cricket field where Len continually exhorted me to assert myself.

It was during my second year in the 1st XI that I first played against Colin Cowdrey, then something of a prodigy at the age of thirteen. Out of a Tonbridge total of barely three figures this plump youth scored 29 not out. A boy called Jackson was bowling big inswingers which had them all in trouble except Cowdrey, whose ability to allow anything not strictly straight to pass harmlessly past the leg stump marked him out as a player of real maturity, even then. His reputation was already made when he played at Christ's Hospital the following year. I can claim to remember few of the wickets I have taken, let alone as long ago as 1946 or 1947, but I do remember hitting the top of his off stump when he had made 12, with a ball that I would have given anything to repeat at will. This time everything went according to plan; after a number of inswingers (with an old ball), I remembered the 'other one' as Len called it, and it pitched about middle stump and hit the top of the off.

Many years later, in 1986, during a pre-Presidential meeting with Colin, when our talk, mainly about Lord's and the future, moved on to cricket in our youth, I asked him, tactlessly perhaps, if he remembered. Unsurprisingly, he did not; after so many innings and centuries for Kent and England later, who could blame him?

In the same season I remember getting Raman Subba Row, then playing for Whitgift, lbw with a ball which after I'd shouted and he had been given out (by their umpire) I realized would probably have missed leg stump. I've never asked Raman if he remembered, though he has often reminded me that playing for Surrey against Essex at Colchester, he was twice caught down the leg side by the wicket-keeper in the same match. Unlucky in any circumstances, but with Jack Bailey the bowler on both occasions, you had to believe that Providence had deserted you.

That some forty years later I should be forced to retire from the field, due partly to the combined efforts of both of them, was a twist of fate which only the Chinese have a word for.

Len Bates left no doubt in my mind that, in his opinion, I had what it needed to become a county cricketer and he took me down to Hove to have this confirmed by Patsy Hendren who was then coach to the Sussex side. At the same time, Len would sometimes take me aside, point from the pitch towards the imposing buildings of the school and murmur, 'Look after yourself over there, won't you?' to remind me of the academic side of life.

The greatest influence on my life at school was without doubt my housemaster, Lionel Carey. He was a very straight man. You always knew where you stood with him and he always expected you to obey his basic rules of manners, directness, integrity and honesty, and to pursue these qualities to the end, regardless. He was, I suppose, an advocate for games-playing Christianity. He spared himself nothing in moulding his charges along good, honest, straightforward lines and expected them to respond with all the effort at their command. Nothing was too much trouble for him. Wise enough to understand people's failings, he would back them to the hilt if they did not deliberately let him down. Money-making activities were all right for some; doubtless even necessary. But his life had been dedicated to service. Although I never felt I could emulate him, I became convinced that a similar way of life was for me, and I decided on a career in teaching with the accent on physical education.

Lionel was steeped in the lore of strict discipline, albeit with a twinkle in his eye for unmalicious offenders. His father had been a housemaster at Sherborne and had been the model for the character Bull in *Loom of Youth*, the novel written by Alec Waugh soon after he had been expelled from the school and which in its time became a *roman-à-clef* of some notoriety. The unfairness of what he saw as an attack both on Sherborne and on his father haunted Lionel, although I never got to know the facts until long after I left school.

By the time I left, to join the Army as a conscript, I had given up any idea of a life in cricket as such. I had an immense love of the game and wanted to continue playing when I could at whatever level, but it was as a schoolmaster that I would earn my living eventually. I had played for Surrey Young Amateurs at The Oval (being qualified for Surrey and Middlesex), had watched the Victory Test match at Lord's and had become firmly convinced that Hammond and Miller were the two greatest cricketers I had ever seen. The sheer magic of watching from the free seats at the Nursery end at Lord's as those two and Hassett, Edrich, Workman, Sismey and the others went their varied ways, led me to make many more visits, once with Len Bates when he talked with all his old friends at the Nursery end, the ground staff and the professionals he had played with, and I was left to marvel at the language and the intimacy of the world of cricket which, I became aware on that occasion, transcended the years.

My two years in the Army were spent largely in the Intelligence Corps, partly in Curzon Street, partly at London headquarters working from offices in the Horse Guards building off Whitehall. It was during this period that I established my first Essex connection when I was introduced by a good friend from school to Buckhurst Hill Cricket Club. I could not have been more fortunate.

Captained by Alan Lavers, an all-rounder good enough to have played for Essex as an amateur off-spinner and middle-order batsman, the club needed an opening bowler. They played in those days on the fringe of Epping Forest on a stretch of ground bordered by the High Road, and the pitch was often lively. I took a fair number of wickets, having been drafted straight into the 1st XI, and the club became the centre of my existence during summer weekends. I played wherever and whenever I could. Alan Lavers proposed me for MCC – I had little idea of the significance of that – and he mentioned me to Essex as a prospect, although nothing came of it at the time.

That first summer the 1st XI had an unbeaten record on the tough Essex club circuit on which former county players and county prospects featured large, and I learned a good deal about batting and bowling against gifted amateurs and about the off-the-field activities which are so much a part of cricket: the beer, the reminiscing, the people. It was while having a good match at the lovely home of the Old Merchant Taylors at Croxley Green that I had a conversation which led to another twist in my life. Several players were undergraduates from Oxford and they asked what my intentions were on leaving the Army. I told them I was going to Loughborough Colleges to train as a teacher.

'You'd get into Oxford easily,' they said, doubtless referring to my cricketing ability rather than my academic prowess. It was as a result of the conversation that followed that I embarked upon a course which was to lead me eventually to University College, Oxford. Almost before I knew it, I was on my way back to Christ's Hospital to see Lionel Carey. I had no Latin – an essential qualification – and my gradings at school had not singled me out as university material, yet Lionel wrote letters. I have no doubt that my eventual securing of a place at University College, having passed the college entrance, although still dependent upon my reaching the required standard of Latin, owed as much to his persuasiveness as to any merit of mine.

Lionel wrote to an old friend of his, H. J. Kittermaster, headmaster of a leading Scottish prep school and a former England rugby international of lasting fame. As a result I spent two years in Edinburgh, teaching at Cargilfield, a leading prep school, and enjoyed every minute of it, far too much to have made any real inroads into the Latin. However, I continued my cricket education by playing on what in those days was one of the best pitches in the country. The Grange CC at Raeburn Place, full of schoolmasters – Guy Willatt, later captain of Derbyshire, once made six successive Sunday hundreds for them – would sometimes see two or three thousand people ringing the boundary, if the sun shone. The Presbyterian Sunday had them in thrall: there was nowhere else to go, no pubs, no cinemas.

The head groundsman would be beside himself if I got the ball above stump height. 'You're destroying my reputation,' he would complain. It was a great place for batsmen and you really earned your wickets. For that reason, like Fenner's or Trent Bridge in the 1950s, it was a marvellous grounding for bowlers.

Eventually I took the best part of a year off and got down to learning the Latin. Back in the south, cramming away, I returned to Buckhurst Hill for my cricket, received a call from Essex, played a few games with some success for the 2nd XI, and was astonished when I was rung up one evening in August.

'How would you like to play for the county at Southend tomorrow?' the voice said. 'Start at 11.30, you would need to be there by 10.30. Can you make it?'

Having thought of the possibility of it being a gigantic leg-pull, I asked a few questions, assured myself that the voice was in fact Horace Clark's, the then Honorary Secretary of Essex, and replied that of course I would play if he was sure I was wanted.

'All expenses will be met,' he said. 'Good luck.'

Although it was thirty-five years ago, I can clearly remember the match, my debut in the first-class game. The new ball was shared by Ken Preston and Ray Smith, the old ball was shared by me, Bill Greensmith . . . and Ray Smith. Ray used to swing with the new ball, his sleeves rolled up, and if 'she was going' there was no better bowler of late swing in the land. When the shine had gone, Ray would generally take a slightly different run and bowl off-spinners, with his sleeves rolled down. I saw comparatively little action as a bowler, six tidy overs for seven runs being my ration in a Nottinghamshire innings that lasted well beyond the tea interval, but I did manage to run out their opening batsman John Clay from extra cover, and that got me into the game.

I mention this match not only because it was my first but because something extraordinary happened when we went out to field for Nottinghamshire's second innings on the second afternoon. Someone in authority had, I believe, talked to Sonny Avery, the Essex senior professional leading the side in place of Doug Insole and the nicest of men. The conversation must have left Sonny in no doubt that I should be given a chance to bowl an extended spell, and probably contained words like 'We've brought him down here to see whether he can bowl, so let's give him a chance'.

I came on as first change when Reg Simpson, the neatest player of quick and other forms of seam bowling you could wish to see, was in full flow. He favoured the back foot and was quick to seize the chance to cut or hook. For a time I did nothing to stem the flow, falling into the error of bowling too short and giving long leg a busy time when Simpson was facing. Yet there was something in the pitch for the off-cutter bowled at pace. The ball bit occasionally and it lifted, and I settled down to a tussle with Reg and his partner. Two short legs, one long leg, a slip and a gully close to the bat, but still no real sign of a breakthrough. Then I remembered Len Bates. What about the 'other one'? I changed the grip and came closer to the stumps, the ball lifted, held its own off the pitch instead of coming in, caught the shoulder of Reg's bat and was pounced on by Sonny Avery, leaning forward in the gully. I had taken my first wicket and Reg Simpson of Nottinghamshire and England had gone for 49.

There are days when things go for you, when you hold the psychological advantage which puts you on top of the world, when you expect to get a wicket with every ball. Now I had three short legs for the right-hander, one in front of square, two behind. Sonny Avery let me have my head. Cyril Poole, the England left-hander, was caught at the wicket off the thinnest of edges. Bruce Dooland, the Australian Test player, was soon out lbw. As Dooland was on his way back to the pavilion I stood there, sweaty and elated. Three wickets. I hadn't disgraced myself.

'Well bowled,' said a voice. And then, after a pause, 'You don't mind me saying that, do you?'

It was Alec Skelding, he of the white boots and pebble glasses, known to give better decisions by instinct than many fellow umpires with far better vision.

'Well bowled,' he said again.

'You can say that as often as you like,' I ventured, with a grin which matched his own roguish smile. There was an unspoken bond between us thereafter. Coming from a man who had seen it all, his words were just the encouragement I needed.

Four more wickets came my way in that innings. I finished with 7 for 32 from seventeen overs, and no single achievement on the cricket field has filled me with more wonder or more joy. My Essex colleagues were all genuinely pleased for me and it says a lot for the game of cricket that nearly all the Nottinghamshire players came into our dressing-room to murmur a quiet 'Well bowled'.

It was heaven. And so, almost uninterrupted, was the rest of that season. From Southend we went to Leicester, from Leicester to Clacton for Essex's last two games. By the end of that season in 1953 I had grown used to the ironic comments of Doug Insole, to rubbing shoulders with England's hero of the day, Trevor Bailey, to being inevitably dubbed by the press as the 'other Bailey'. I had also taken 25 wickets in four matches at 13 each and, when the final national averages were published, there I was, perched at the top of the list. It was, perhaps, a fitting commentary on this that Bill Johnston, the Australian left-arm bowler, and no batsman, finished top of the batting averages.

It was good while it lasted. I played regularly for Essex the following season, still glancing at the odd book prior to going to Oxford, and I loved every minute and was not unsuccessful.

I quickly found out, however, that the fresh, unseen bowler has an advantage which has virtually disappeared by the time he meets the same opposition on the second occasion. Wickets are harder to come by than during that first, careless rapture. I took about 80 wickets at 18 each in the following season, a tally uncannily and accurately forecast early in the summer by Jim Laker. I played as much cricket as I could, wherever I could, and prepared myself for going up to university in 1955.

That 1954 season was one of learning about the county game, the circuit, the do's and don'ts, the umpires, the mythology. I learned, too, of Doug Insole's ability as a player and as captain. He suited the Essex team and its ambience; his neo-cockney sense of humour, penchant for devastating one-liners, plus his shrewd common sense on the field, enabled him to make the best of a team which, attractively though it played, was never well enough equipped to find its way out of the bottom half of the table. That fine all-rounder Trevor Bailey was often pre-occupied with England duties, but was obviously a great asset when he was fit and on song. Insole himself was so unorthodox a batsman that the purist would never pick him if he saw him in the nets and did not know who he was, how many runs he had scored. But effective he certainly was; a doughty and cour-ageous performer. Extremely nervous when Essex were batting, he was also highly superstitious; you dared not move from your seat for *any* reason when a stand was in progress. Those were the days too of Dickie Dodds, Sonny Avery, Paul Gibb, Dick Horsfall, Ray Smith, Bill Greensmith, Ken Preston.

Virtually every Essex home match was an away match as we pitched tents for no more than a week in any one place and made our way round the circuit of Chelmsford, Brentwood, Southend, Colchester, Westcliff, Clacton and, occasionally, Leyton. Brian Castor, a former Secretary of Essex but then Secre-tary at The Oval, compiled the county fixture lists. He had no assistance, not even from computers, and generally did a highly competent job. Essex, however, was somewhat out on a limb and we became used to long car journeys, often arriving at the next venue on the wrong side of midnight. One chunk of three fixtures tested even our powers of endurance. To make the point we sent Brian Castor a postcard from each. 'It's lovely here at Clacton', the first read. 'Lovely here at Weston-super-Mare', said the second. We posted the third from Scarborough.

Perhaps because it was all so new to me, perhaps because it was not my living, I enjoyed every moment, including the travelling. Being on the inside of the great game was enough. And Oxford beckoned. Before my one full season with Essex was at an end, I had another memorable encounter with my favourite umpire, Alec Skelding. It took place off the field. Surrey versus Essex at The Oval: I arrived early and made my way to the amateur dressing-room, as it then was, high up in the pavilion, replete with its luxurious wickerwork armchairs, massage table and wash basins. Only one other person was there: Alec Skelding. He was shaving, with a cut-throat razor. His pebble glasses rested by the side of the table, he squinted in the mirror. We exchanged greetings.

'Good morning, Mr Skelding.'

'Good morning.'

'Isn't it rather dangerous, shaving with that cut-throat razor? And without your glasses?'

'Well, to tell the truth, I had rather more than I meant to last night. My hand is rather shaky. I took off my glasses because I can't stand the sight of blood.' He was irrepressible.

It was during that same match (not, I firmly believe, as is often reported, a match between Surrey and The Rest) that the Insole gift for the apt and pithy comment reached its zenith. In those days The Oval was nothing if not a joy for the likes of Bedser, Loader, Lock and Laker. It was near the end of a day's play. Essex were in trouble. The light was fading. Essex lost a wicket and it was just about light enough for Insole to go in. A few balls later he was out, bowled Lock. Two stumps lay flat on the ground. England's slow left-arm bowler had struck again, but this time with a ball of which Peter Loader would have been proud. It was no secret that Lockie's arm straightened at the point of delivery, especially when he let loose his quicker ball. Later, he and a number of others in the first-class game were forced to remodel their actions. Here, playing for Surrey against Essex, he was free of all inhibitions. As Insole surveyed his wrecked wicket there was no doubt in his mind that the ball had been thrown.

'How was I out, then?' he called to the square-leg umpire. 'Run out?'

I remember a Soho dinner with Raman Subba Row during that match. At that time my interest in the game did not extend beyond the futures of Essex and England, my own performances and those of my contemporaries. But even then Raman was talking of the game's future and what he saw as its current malaise. It was to be a long time before we found ourselves addressing similar topics again.

During my three years at Oxford (having first satisfied the examiners in Latin and having obtained a grant from the good old London County Council), it was cricket, rugby and work, regrettably in that order. I did enough in the library and lecture-rooms to keep my nose clean, borrowed M. J. K. Smith's notes on certain subjects which he had appeared to have covered more comprehensively than I, and during my first year played under him in the Oxford XI. M.J.K. had the unique distinction of scoring a century in each of his three University matches, one of them a double hundred. As a captain, he was somewhat diffident in approach, a man of comparatively few words, but tactically sound. He was straight. My fellow opening bowler in 1956 was Esmond Kentish, who had played for West Indies and Jamaica, had taken 10 wickets in a Test match against England and was thirty-eight years old. He was on a one-year diploma course and was a tremendous asset to us. We became firm friends and room-mates when the pre-University match tour was underway. M.J.K.'s captaincy was tested at Worcester when Esmond, who naturally enough had choice of ends, opted to bowl the first over into the wind. Smith was puzzled. 'Why this end, Esmond?' he asked. 'It's blowing half a gale this way'.

Esmond explained that I had been out late the night before (which I had, with the captain's permission) and he felt that I should have the wind behind me. Smith's answer was unprintable, and I bowled into the wind.

The University match meant something in the mid-1950s. Oxford and Cambridge were still supplying cricketers and administrators thick and fast to England and to Lord's. It was also something of a social occasion. It was not uncommon for more than 10,000 people to come to watch the match on that first Saturday in July. Esmond confessed to me that he had never been so nervous, not even in a Test match, as he was that first morning at Lord's, under the watchful but, to us, benevolent eye of the President of Oxford University Cricket Club, D. R. Jardine. Douglas Jardine appeared to us to have been a much maligned man. His generosity, wise counsel and advice were always at hand if we needed it; and if we were in awe of him, we were also full of admiration and respect. Another spectator on that day was the great Sir Donald Bradman. History does not record whether they met or what they said if they did. I do know, however, that the Don was not greatly impressed by our bowling, which, following a conversation between M. J. K. Smith and Douglas Jardine, was directed largely at the leg stump.

None of the three University matches that I played in produced much that was entertaining in the cricket. In my final year, as captain, we bowled all day on the Saturday, apart from an hour lost to rain, while Cambridge scored 132 for 7 wickets. We bowled well and the fielding was excellent but Cambridge, with Ted Dexter as my opposite number and with five others who went on to play for their county or Australian State sides, did not do themselves justice. The double weight of the tradition of both University and Lord's took a deal of shifting from the shoulders. To us it was the Ashes and the need to play attractive cricket has not dawned on us.

The middle and late 1950s were still nurturing times for sport at Oxford and Cambridge. The screw was tightening, almost imperceptibly, but the crazy attitude of prowess at sport becoming a positive handicap to gaining admission was still over the horizon. It was always necessary in my time to satisfy the examiners, but there was ample scope for other activities. Indeed they were encouraged and expected.

A Blue was of value both within the university and outside. It meant something; and if it was gained for cricket or rugby football it was seen as a first-class achievement. In both sports, the two universities were still looked on as cradles for the international game. Indeed it was rare for Oxford rugby, with its cosmopolitan population, with its Rhodes Scholars selected for their all-round prowess, not to be able to call up at least one player of ready-made international standing. My first year at Oxford saw me playing for the Greyhounds at centre three-quarter, but, short of an epidemic of some kind, with no real hope of getting a Blue for rugby. Those were the days of Allaway, the Rhodesian hooker, who captained Oxford with verve and with innovation and with the sheer pluck to stick to breath-taking unorthodoxy as Oxford nailed like a banner to their mast the use of the scissors and dummy-scissors moves. There was Onlwyn Brace of Wales at scrum-half, whose speed from the base of the scrum made him the unusual pivot of the attack; M. J. K. Smith with his cricketer's hands and mighty kick was at fly-half; John Currie of England was in the second row of the scrum; and Roy Plumbridge from South Africa, Peter Robbins, later an England stalwart, and Robin Davies of Wales formed the Oxford back row. The individual was subordinate to the scheme, the scheme one of bewildering sleight of hand when the ball came to the backs. Side after side was wrong-footed, literally, and one after the other swept away by the daring and boldness and skill of it all.

None of it would have been possible without the ability to train virtually every afternoon at Iffley Road. Familiarity with each other was everything and only at Oxford or Cambridge in those days was the 'professional' approach to an essentially amateur game possible. No other club had the time. That year was breathtaking in its scope and audacity and I was honoured to be selected in the 2nd XV match when we beat a Cambridge LX Club team, containing E. R. Dexter, by a handy margin. Cambridge, the great enemy, went the way of all flesh when Allaway's team encountered them at Twickenham.

In those days most of us had done a couple of years of National Service. We were consequently that much stronger and more experienced, less easily intimidated. But whereas rugby-playing undergraduates held a distinct advantage in an amateur game, the same was not at all true of the cricket world. There was little or nothing we could teach the county professional, except perhaps enthusiasm. Here the boot was entirely on the other foot. The chief joy came from playing against and learning from the great men of the game, giving them a run for their money and occasionally, just occasionally, more than they had bargained for. Then there was the joy of playing in the Parks. The Parks at Oxford is arguably the most enchanting ground on which first-class cricket is played in England. Early summer, when trees of every possible hue ringed the ground, made you glad to be alive and privileged to be part of the scene where famous deeds had been done in the name of Oxford University.

My own first summer playing for the University saw us struggling for survival against the giants from the north. Trueman and Statham, loosening up for the season ahead, Tattersall, Malcolm Hilton, Appleyard, Wardle, were all keen to make a good start to the campaign of the next four months, while we, like so many new-born foals, struggled to find our feet.

Then there came a match against the young Ingleby-Mackenzie's Hampshire. It was one of the best in which I have ever played. There had been no need for declarations, and at the start of the third day Oxford needed 305 runs to win on a good but wearing wicket. By the time our last man, Esmond Kentish, came to the wicket to face the last ball, the match could have gone any of four ways. Thanks largely to our middle order, in which Michael Eagar, cousin of the then Hampshire Secretary, Desmond, had played a starring role with his wristy, hockey-player's strokes on both sides of the wicket, Oxford had reached 303 for 9. Two to win, one to draw. Unthinkably, if the last wicket fell to that one remaining ball, Oxford could lose or, in the event of a run-out on the second run, tie the match. Esmond Kentish had not been overwhelmed with advice before he came to the wicket; that was not Mike Smith's style. The unerringly accurate Vic Cannings bowled the last ball at his brisk medium pace. As usual it was just short of a length. Esmond, lost in the moment, forgot all that his great experience had taught him and swung mightily towards mid-wicket, before turning to survey his shattered wicket. Oxford had come within a whisker of taking their first county scalp for five years. But so enthralled had we all been by the perfect match that the result seemed far less important than the knowledge that we were good enough to do it. That season, 1956, did eventually bring wins over Gloucestershire and Warwickshire and those victories owed much to that Hampshire match and the feeling of confidence it gave us.

Matches against tourists in those days were played chiefly at Christ Church, the Parks being sacrosanct for money-making purposes and no gate being possible to help meet the tourists' expenses. In 1956 we played the Australians; in 1957 the West Indians. On both occasions the pitch was low and slow. On both occasions the touring team were serious in intent, building towards the strenuous season ahead. We were outclassed, but we gave a reasonable account of ourselves, certainly doing well enough to make both teams aware that they had been in a worthwhile match.

The 1957 West Indies team, with Ramadhin and Valentine, bowled us out cheaply in the first innings of the match in spite of an innings of the highest class by Chris Walton, our captain, a fine player who at Radley had lived under the shadow of Ted Dexter. Ramadhin had perplexed better players than us and was largely instrumental in reducing the University to a total which barely reached the three-figure mark. Of the three Ws the West Indies batting contained only Clyde Walcott, and he made a half century of power and beauty. I can remember still the elation which ran through the Oxford team when we had five West Indians out – including Walcott himself and Collie Smith who had earlier hit the new ball for 6 over long-on. At the wicket were the reserve wicket-keeper and a slow left-arm bowler, batting at numbers 7 and 8. The ball was still moving about, but it was no time before the bowling was made to look ordinary. The full face of the bat was presented with time and to spare. The scoreboard rattled away. It was Kanhai and Sobers at the wicket, each on the threshold of their great careers.

Working out Ramadhin's spin was less difficult from the pavilion, or from behind the arm, than it was when you were out there in the arena. Roy Woodcock, our slow left-arm bowler and a useful middle-order batsman, had stayed around for a time in the first innings without making too many runs, and he returned to the pavilion certain that he had worked out the leg-break and the off-break, bowled from the front of the hand by Ramadhin in a way not seen before or since. As we prepared to follow on from our first innings, Roy explained it with the greatest confidence and I, for one, was impressed. Less impressive, though, was the sight of Roy shouldering arms to Ramadhin's off-break early in his second innings, with the inevitable result. Roy Woodcock later ran the cricket at Charterhouse with considerable success; I doubt whether his recollections of his first-class career often referred to this particular moment on rainy afternoons at the school.

He was one of those who accompanied me into my third year playing for Oxford, but that 1958 season saw few other seniors taking their place in the XI. There was a promising rash of freshmen, though, and I found the task of captaining the team an unalloyed pleasure. Unalloyed when I was actually doing it, that is. The problems of captaincy of the Oxford XI lay chiefly with the coincidence of final examinations in the same term. This meant carrying a heavy burden on two fronts. When playing, the formula for the day was a wearing one. Up at 5.30 a.m.; work from 6 until 10 with a gap for breakfast half-way; off to the Parks on the ramshackle bike to arrive more than an hour before the start. A quiet moment or two came next, to think some rudimentary thoughts about the coming day's play. Often this would be combined with a brief talk with Mr Leach, the grizzled old retainer, much revered, who looked after the dressing-rooms and – luxury of luxuries – cleaned the boots and whitened the pads. At the end of the day's play, a couple of beers with the boys and the opposition, off home for something to eat and then, if not totally exhausted, having bowled twenty-odd overs, a couple of hours more work.

Mr Leach was a mine of information if he liked you and you were prepared to talk and listen to him. He had his own firm ideas about cricket and cricketers. Colin Cowdrey was a fine player, so was M. J. K. Smith and Donald Carr before him. 'But there was one player in my day, sir, who was in a class of his own. None of the others come near him. Mr Donnelly was far and away the best player we've had here since the war.' Martin Donnelly of Oxford, Warwickshire and New Zealand was the number one batsman in Mr Leach's book and for all I know he never changed his mind.

It was Mr Leach who came up to me one day in the middle of my first term while it was still uncertain what the opening attack would be. I had already played with some success for Essex, but was by no means sure of my place. There was Esmond Kentish, quicker than anyone and already a Test player. There was a Blue from the previous year in John Phillips, a whole-hearted performer. Also highly regarded was Richard Bowman who later played for Lancashire, fast and with plenty of raw talent; and there was me. It was certain that one, probably two, of us would not be in the team for Lord's, and for a time the competition was fierce. Mr Leach tried to set my mind at rest. 'Will you play for me at Lord's, sir?' he asked, when I was in the dressing-room and nobody else within earshot. Somewhat bemused, I said I'd be delighted, and thought little more about the conversation. A week or so later, Mike Smith asked me the same question. How old Leach did it, I don't know – perhaps he overheard things during his daily rounds and put two and two together. Perhaps his instincts were uncannily accurate. Whatever the reasons, Mr Leach, as I later found out, asked a similar question of all those chosen that year and the next, and the next, and always well in advance of the official invitation.

It was wet that summer of 1958 and the Parks pitches were open to the elements. With me in the attack I had a freshman called David Sayer of Kent, who bowled as fast as anyone around in those days, except perhaps Tyson, Trueman and Statham. Another freshman, Dan Piachaud, who later played for Hampshire, had a smooth flowing action which gave his off-spinners a lovely curling loop. Andrew Curran, who later captained Notts and was our third seamer; the wicket-keeper, Alan Smith from Warwickshire, later to be Secretary of TCCB; and Javed Burki, later to captain Pakistan, were all freshmen. Martin Dyson, Mike Eagar, Dick Jowett and Ian Gibson were seniors who worthily gained their places in the team against Cambridge, as did Roy Woodcock, another old Blue. Ian Gibson was a wayward genius of an opening bat who also boasted a fizzing leg-break.

The strength of our attack in the prevailing conditions of that summer was such that the county circuit was quickly aware that Oxford was no place for a quiet outing and a gentle knock to bolster the batting average. Our batting was less formidable, though we sold our wickets dearly.

I suppose the highlight of the season was the dismissal of the touring New Zealanders in their second innings for 45 runs in under two hours, after they had scored well over 300 in their first. David Sayer and I bowled unchanged and we were supported by some of the finest close-catching I have seen. Everything worked. It was one of those days when each time I changed the field it had the desired effect. We failed in our attempt to knock off the 150 or so runs needed for victory, but by the end of that last day's play the Parks, once virtually empty, was thronged with dons and undergraduates, word having gone round that something unusual was afoot and some sort of history might be in the making. Though we had to settle for a draw, we had certainly had our moments and it was a game I shall always remember.

And we went on having them, at intervals; so that when we took on Ted Dexter's Cambridge team at Lord's that year, we entertained real hopes of ending a sequence of six University matches without an Oxford win. We failed, and it was left to Alan Smith, with most of the same team, but with the addition of the Nawab of Pataudi and Abbas Ali Baig, both of whom later played with great distinction for India, to bring home the bacon. Bacon, I like to think, had at least been cured by our experiences of 1958.

It was while I was at Oxford that I made my first decisive contact with MCC and what it then stood for. I received a letter at the beginning of my final year from Ronny Aird, then Secretary, asking if I would be available to tour that December/January 1957–58. MCC were going to East Africa for four weeks and the Committee would like to know. . . . It was like a message from Olympus.

I was to visit East Africa, South America and then Canada and the United States, representing the Marylebone Cricket Club all in the space of two years, and I was captured for the Club for evermore. The certainty and courtesy with which everything was arranged, the aura of those MCC initials in over-seas cricket circles, and the happiness of the players on those tours, left an indelible mark.

Major tours under MCC's banner – to Australia, West Indies, New Zealand and so on – come much more under the glare of the spotlight, but even in the 1950s and 1960s it was performance on the field, rather than off it, which found its way into the newspapers or filtered over the air. Tours can still be fun, though. Politics and the immediacy of the media, the probing eye of television and the changed priorities of pretty well all the editors of British national dailies, led on it seems by the lowest common denominators, may have taken some of the gilt from the gingerbread, but in cricket much more of the good is left over from the 'bad old days' than in most sports.

It has to be said, however, that increased speed of communication has taken away much of the glamour which used to be a product of the imagination. The sheer inaccessability of places like India and Australia made radio commentaries over the distant, crackling air a special ingredient of cold hard winters at home. The imagination could take wing; cricket heroes were that much larger; the mystique of the game and of the players at the highest level were more easily preserved. There was more room for the romantically inclined. In many ways cricket was the richer for it. However, the shrinking of the world has brought with it many advantages for the game. Politicians permitting, more parts of the globe are visited more often by more teams, at all levels, than ever before. Universities, schools, ordinary club sides, as well as those with grander labels, now tread well worn paths to the furthest corners. Teams from other countries pass through Lord's in the English summer with pleasing regularity on their way round England. More general aspects of life than mere cricket benefit.

It has long been MCC's policy to send teams to every part of the globe where cricket is played, not just at international level, but anywhere a visit can be rewarding in terms of furthering the game. There have been, for example, three tours to Bangladesh since the mid-1970s. Each team contained a number of stalwart campaigners, ex-England players and the like, who had been used to touring in relatively luxurious conditions, yet, having encountered a much more primitive state of affairs and an arduous itinerary, returned home talking of the best tour ever.

The tour to East Africa in 1957–58 was the first of several I was lucky enough to accompany as either player or as manager. At Oxford at the time, and in some doubt as to whether I could accept because of the pressures of work, which was not coming especially easily, I consulted my tutor and the Dean of my college who, wise as they were, insisted that it would be a worthwhile experience, not to be missed. Even if it did take up all the vacation there would still be some time left for the books; and anyway, wasn't I reading geography?

So I assembled along with twelve cricketers of varying ages and experience at the London Air Terminal on Boxing Day, 1957. We were flying to Dar-es-Salaam. There was snow on the ground. The flight was scheduled to take thirty-six hours and we were due to play the day after arrival against a Tanganyikan XI. The captain was F. R. Brown; the vice-captain, S. C. Griffith, later to be Secretary of MCC. Other members of the team, who had no more idea of what awaited us than I had, were M. J. K. Smith (Oxford University and Warwickshire), P. E. Richardson (Worcestershire, Kent and England), A. C. D. Ingleby-Mackenzie (later captain of Hampshire), G. H. G. Doggart (Cambridge University, Sussex and England), D. R. W. Silk (Cambridge University and Somerset), G. W. Cook (Cambridge University), C. J. M. Kenny (Cambridge University and Essex), J. J. Warr (Cambridge University, Middlesex and England) and R. V. C. Robins (Middlesex). The tour was to last a month and there was no doubt, even at this stage, that the team had been selected as much with an eye to the bonhomie it was likely to engender as to its considerable potential on the field.

BOAC (as British Airways was then) used Argonauts on the East African run. None of your streamlined jet comfort, but a happy antiquity and a friendly crew and the steady drone of the engines as they slowly but surely took us, via Madrid, over the shimmering heat of the North African desert. Thirty-six hours in an aeroplane could not have passed more happily. The in-jokes of seasoned England tourists held us lesser members of the party enthralled, and for someone making his first flight of any kind there was a curiosity in all that happened. We finally arrived at Dar-es-Salaam at 9 p.m. local time and went our various ways with our colonial hosts and crawled under the mosquito netting conscious of the humidity, but only just; aware of the lizards dotted around the walls and ceilings, but only just; for tiredness quickly had the final word.

There was no doubt about the climate or our surroundings when we reached the ground the following morning in good time for a 10.30 start. It was so hot and humid that even the locals remarked upon it. We were short of practice, so we limbered up. We soon found that the heat and the humidity left us short of breath, and we were glad when a halt was called and the captain went to toss. A few silent prayers were offered for his wisdom in selecting the right side of whatever coin it was. The matting wicket glimmered in the sun. If only we could win the toss, pile up a score, become acclimatized. . . . The captain returned, full of smiles. He had won the toss (sighs of relief) and he had put them in (gasps of horror). Good reasons there were, but after an hour or two out there against a competent team our party began to take on the aspect of a casualty clearing station. The wicket was true, the batsmen were soon humming 'I've grown accustomed to your pace' . . . and swiftly the physical effects of the humidity manifested themselves. Billy Griffith, our wicket-keeper, was soon halting the bowler in mid-run with the cry, 'I don't think cover-point is quite ready.' This proved to be a mild understatement, for cover-point had his back to the game and was retching violently.

Another of our number almost simultaneously developed a continuous nose-bleed which necessitated his removal from the field. This depletion in our side was not further helped by the fact that the twelfth man, Dennis Silk, was under the influence of flu. Yet he came out, took a brilliant catch at a crucial time in the Tanganyikan innings and as much as anyone else enabled us finally to escape with a hard-earned draw.

It was a tour wherein all sorts of adaptations to climatic conditions were necessary. From the low-lying, humid Dar-es-Salaam, we moved to the altitude of Nairobi with its thin air and the consequent breathlessness of our quicker bowlers – solved in part by the captain using them in pairs from one end, so that they took alternate overs and thus each bowled only one over in three, while a slow bowler was wheeling away at the other end.

Today's club and school tourists will be fitter and younger than some of us were. But they will still enjoy the good times in each other's company that we had, and every cricket touring side has. More quickly than anything they will discover the strengths, weaknesses and peculiarities of their companions. Jokes and nicknames will abound from the tour wit (there always is one) and time will go along very, very quickly. Above all they will enjoy that special feeling which comes from being strangers in a strange land where everyone wants to extend the hand of friendship and hospitality. For a few weeks they will see the best of everything and be treated much like kings. All that remains is for them to perform royally on and off the field.

Apart from short forays into Holland and Denmark, I went on several other tours with MCC, and managed two, one to East Africa again, with Michael Brearley as captain, and one to the Far East, this time skippered by Colin Ingleby-Mackenzie. The magic of Marylebone extended throughout the world and all who took part came to realize, if they had not already done so (and most of them had), that there was more to touring under the old red and yellow flag than simply playing cricket. There was a need to encourage, a need to put yourselves out if called on so that your hosts always felt you welcomed their entertainment no matter how much you may have wanted to crawl into bed.

After Oxford, I taught for two hugely enjoyable years at Bedford School, where I ran the cricket. Then with a young family to support and feeling the need to earn more than I could possibly get from schoolmastering, I joined the Reed Paper Group (now Reed International), spending Saturdays writing on cricket and rugby football for the *Sunday Telegraph*. Throughout the years my links with MCC were maintained through playing, writing about or watching cricket, or using the nets at Lord's. The Club and I became the firmest of friends.

2

CLOSE ENCOUNTERS

MY INTRODUCTION INTO the world of cricket administration could be described as out of the Clark Report of
1966 and by a number of sires including David Clark himself,
Chairman of the Clark Report committee, Billy Griffith then
Secretary of MCC, the Warwickshire Supporters' Association
and a sprinkling of county executives. The birth was Caesarean.

The idea of someone with the prime duties of looking after
the press, public relations and the business side of cricket had met
with considerable opposition. The counties refused it once; and
there was some initial reluctance within MCC itself, where
Gubby Allen, then Treasurer, was virtually all-powerful.
Finally, after a year in which Dennis Morris from the BBC had
scrutinized the scene and had initiated several notable improvements to the public face of the game, I was appointed. I took
up my duties in July 1967.

The post was described as an 'additional assistant secretary
of MCC with particular responsibilities for press and public relations'. In practice, this meant a hell of a lot of work for the

Club itself, including looking after the ground, MCC's own fixture list of 180 matches, the press, certain aspects of the Club's finances, and much more besides. In addition, there was a whole field wide open for progress within cricket at large. The monumental task that lay ahead had been outlined in the Clark Report. So had the reasons for it.

David Clark and his distinguished committee had studied a mountain of evidence, had met and met again and had produced an extensive report. The plain fact was that English cricket at county level was in the doldrums. The clubs presumably recognized that continually dwindling gates at Test and county level, declining membership figures and lacklustre performances on indifferently prepared pitches went hand in hand with a decline in prosperity, but nevertheless a majority disagreed with the proposed cures.

Among the remedies put forward by Clark and his men were: the reduction of the three-day county championship to sixteen matches, a separate championship of sixteen one-day matches, the speedy introduction into county teams of overseas players, the examination of commercial sponsorship, and the appointment of someone to look after press and public relations.

The unexpected letter from Billy Griffith in the summer of 1966, asking if I would like to be considered for that post, presented me with several problems on a personal level. At this stage of my career I had been employed for some half-dozen years by Reed, had been promoted a couple of times and was firmly wedded to my weekend writing for the *Sunday Telegraph* on cricket and rugby. Furthermore, I was in the throes of making a big decision. Reed had asked if I would be prepared to go to Trinidad as general manager for a new venture to be set up by themselves and Rugby Portland Cement and I had indicated that I would be very interested. It was a step upwards and presented a considerable challenge. There was no doubt that the job was mine if I wanted it.

The letter from MCC arrived just in time for me to be able to withdraw from the Trinidad job with honour, but I had to burn those particular boats before knowing for certain that the cricket job was mine. In a triumph of heart over mind I made myself available to Lord's, went for a satisfactory interview, discussed the terms and the salary, carried on with my old job at Reed and then . . . hey presto, there was no job to go to. The counties were persuaded that they didn't yet want someone in a permanent capacity conforming to the job description given, but they were prepared to let Dennis Morris have a look at the task and prepare a report.

I continued with my old job with Reed, disappointed but philosophical. It was with some surprise about a year later that I received another call from Lord's. Was I still available? Another conflict, this time tinged with a feeling of once bitten, twice shy. 'Was there really a job?' Yes, I would be assistant secretary. I could continue to write on rugby, but in the circumstances cricket for the *Sunday Telegraph* was out. Initially my salary would be paid with the help of money provided by the Warwickshire Supporters' Association (courtesy of the Warwickshire CCC football pool).

I made another decision, instinctive rather than from a cool long-term appraisal. Knowing that I would be financially worse off as a result, with a wife and three children, but with the support of my wife Julianne, I was on my way to Lord's. The truth was that I was enamoured of the game, the philosophy it expressed and the vast majority of the people in it.

As someone who had played cricket for Oxford University and Essex, had kept in touch with the game through writing about it and had been on three MCC tours; had enjoyed every moment of every visit to Lord's and had sniffed the air with relish every time I slipped through the Grace Gates, the thought of working for MCC was heady stuff. I knew little of the complexities of cricket administration, of the hierarchical structure of Lord's itself, of the hours of tactful persuasion needed to accomplish the smallest objective as the committee system batted ideas to and fro.

I was soon to learn the problems involved in serving two

different masters – the counties on the one hand, MCC on the other. It was not that the essential interests of either party conflicted. It was just that in those early days what I had thought were the terms of my appointment had proved to be wide of the mark. I had much to learn about the sheer cussedness of human nature where a religion like cricket was involved, and for some time I spread myself too thinly and was in danger of achieving little, in spite of long hours at the expense of my family and inevitable weekends spent at the job. But all these routine worries were soon overshadowed as I became involved in my first cricket *cause célèbre* before I had really found my bearings. The Brian Close affair was upon us.

If you look in *Wisden* for the year of 1968 (covering the events of the 1967 season), you will find mention of strange happenings involving Brian Close, captain of England and of Yorkshire; but these allusions are matter-of-fact, almost bland. They are restricted in scope and confined to the appropriate part of the 'bible'. In passing, the bald facts are mentioned. Yorkshire, on 18 August, achieved a draw against Warwickshire at Edgbaston. Warwickshire, needing 142 runs to win in 100 minutes, failed by 9 runs. During this 100 minutes, Yorkshire bowled only twenty-four overs; and only two overs in the last fifteen minutes. A draw gave them two valuable points although, as it turned out later, these were not significant in Yorkshire's Championship win.

It was a prima-facie case of a breach of the Law governing fair and unfair play: blatant time-wasting. There were also allegations of jostling between Brian Close and some Warwickshire members, although these remained accusations and nothing of substance was ever established.

As a very new boy, I was impressed with the speed and thoroughness of the subsequent investigation. That Brian Close had incurred the wrath of the Establishment was obvious some time before the enquiry took place. All sorts of people including the then Duke of Norfolk had been on the telephone. It was evident that 'Closey' was on a hiding to nothing unless some pretty surprising developments took place at the last moment. None did.

Meanwhile the mail landed with a thump on my desk. The telephone calls never ceased. Brian Close was no ordinary cricketer, and this incident had occurred at a particularly contentious time. It should be remembered that Close was a highly successful captain of England. He was also champion of the north, the epitome of the professional approach, the straight-shooting, straight-talking Yorkshire pro who had transformed the England team from an apparently rudderless coaster into a briskly-manoeuvred, well-equipped destroyer. In the last match of the 1966 series against the West Indies, Close had replaced Colin Cowdrey as captain. I had been at The Oval as an ordinary onlooker, and had witnessed a new aggressiveness, a refusal to submit, whatever the odds might appear to be. The early introduction of Bob Barber's leg-spin, the crowding of the batsmen, including the prolific Garfield Sobers, struck a welcome note. A fresh determination was in the air and it made its own luck. The West Indies were beaten by England for the first time that summer. Now, in 1967, having led England while they defeated India, and due to go into the final Test against Pakistan one match ahead in the three-match series, Close was an unbeaten captain of England when 'Edgbaston' came tumbling about his ears. Until then, he had been certain to take the MCC team to the Caribbean.

Close's arraignment should also be seen against the back-drop of other decisions by the establishment which had earned the ire and scorn of certain sections of the press. Those were the days of Michael Parkinson for the *Sunday Times*: the days of writings which championed the cause of the common man, especially the Yorkshire common man, and reviled those 'port swilling' committee men at Lord's. The fire had been fuelled early in the 1967 season by the dropping of Boycott after he had made 246 not out, albeit slowly, in the first Test match of the season against India. When Close was found guilty then of time-wasting and severely censured, it was seen by some as another miscarriage of justice at the hands of the southern, public-school, Oxbridge brigade. It was an unfair assessment. It was untrue, certainly in so far as conscious motives were concerned. But the critics were quick to point out that in those days (before the Law which made it mandatory to bowl twenty overs in the last hour, or else carry on playing), there had been several reported cases of time-wasting and none had been given the same weight by those in authority.

So when, on the very eve of the Test at The Oval against Pakistan, a hearing was held at Lord's and it was known that the MCC Committee would be considering the findings before the captain for the West Indies tour was announced, Brian Close was put under great strain.

Picture the scene. The next day he was due to captain England. His car broke down on the way to the hearing. He was late. He was bothered and he seemed genuinely bewildered. Reasonably enough, he was, as captain of Yorkshire, held responsible for his team's time-wasting tactics. It was my job to draft a brief press statement. The announcement was delayed until after the Test match, but it was simple and stark: Mr Close had been severely reprimanded for his part in the Edgbaston affair.

Brian knew this as he led England to an eight-wicket victory. He must also have known that his captaincy of the team to go to the West Indies that winter was in jeopardy. The MCC Committee were to consider the appointment during the Test itself. Whether he could have saved himself by a written apology is doubtful. It probably did not occur to him that this would have the desired affect; he was not skilled at diplomacy or face-saving gestures. In any case, he was just as likely to take literally the advice of Brian Sellers, the Yorkshire Chairman, after the enquiry to put all that behind him and get on wi' t'job. That is just what he did, during that final Test match.

The fact that he did not apologize is quoted against Close, the impression being given that this was almost as big a crime as the time-wasting itself. I just do not think he could have saved himself. The moving finger, having writ, was already moving on, pointing a return to the more familiar school of England captaincy: the less successful, cleverly self-effacing, supremely diplomatic one epitomized by Colin Cowdrey. The Committee were determined to uphold the principle of fair play on the field and to be seen to be doing it; and in their eyes the removal of Close was the inevitable outcome.

Poor old Closey – described by the *Washington Post* (yes, the *Washington Post*) as upright of bearing, with bemused, crumpled features – had his supporters. The chairman of selectors, Douglas Insole, was one of them. He remained in support of Close as England's captain right to the end.

To someone brand new to cricket administration and dropped straight in at the deep end, it was a shot–gun education. One of the first things that struck me was the breadth of knowledge of the MCC Committee at the time. Sir Alec Douglas Home was President; industry, politics, cricket administration, education and the law were among the pursuits represented at the highest level. The atmosphere at meetings was kindly, courteous, attentive, sincere, and decisions were taken in the light of the best professional advice available. The highest standards prevailed. The great club was involved not only in every aspect of the game, but was at the centre of all decisions affecting it both at home and internationally. The Secretariat, with G. O. Allen the Treasurer, were at the very core of this centre. The workload was tremendous. We kept running to stand still. Yet sometime, somehow, the ailing patient called English first-class cricket had to be revived and the approach required to achieve it had to be thoroughly professional.

Tinkering with the Laws in order to make the game more attractive was of little use if the fundamentals were wrong. And the fundamentals at this stage of the game's history had more to do with the fact that cricket was no longer reflecting the social climate in which we lived. The game at first-class level was heading slowly towards the status of an anachronism. It was in decline at the top level because it was barely competing for the hearts and minds of the people. The faithful still followed, but a new generation of agnostics was upon us and the need for conversion was urgent.

The Clark Report had pointed to a number of failings, and much of what had been recommended had been laced with good common sense. But the majority of counties had come out against it. Everyone agreed that the first-class game was desperately short of money. Everyone recognized that the current programme of county matches and Test matches was attracting progressively fewer people through the gates. Yet nobody could agree on how to resolve the problem. It became clear to me that a large part of my job was to convince the counties and of course MCC that more money could be obtained, to convince them of how it could be obtained, even under existing circumstances (which were not ideal), and to point to changes which, if effected, could attract enough money to make a thoroughly professional game, as it now was in England, relatively solvent. It had become necessary to make money to be able to continue to play cricket. But if we were to make it, something had to give.

The obvious target was the traditional Sunday day of rest.

The Clark Committee had recommended that three-day county championship matches be played over weekends, with the second day on Sundays. In order to avoid public censure and the wrath of the Lord's Day Observance Society, and so as not to compete with Sunday morning church-going, the second day's play started at 2.00 p.m. It was terribly truncated, and what cricket there was often resulted in tedium. The Sunday crowds dwindled. Instances of grounds emptying before the close of play were not uncommon. The prospects were bleak.

In stark contrast were the activities of teams not taking part in a championship match. While the county game languished, the same players were providing meat and drink to the cricket-loving public in limited-over matches (40 overs per team) played on a county ground, usually as part of a player's benefit and, what is more, televised on BBC2, sponsored by Rothmans and organized by an agent of many of the household names in cricket, past and present: Dexter, Graveney, Sobers, T. E. Bailey, Compton, Laker, Cowdrey, to name a few. The Rothmans Cavaliers, as they were called, became a household name through their exposure on BBC2 every Sunday afternoon, and good luck to them. But while the individual beneficiary of the county club involved on the day did well out of the match, the larger interests of the game benefited hardly at all.

For someone who was employed to look after the best interests of cricket as a whole, here was food for thought. As things turned out, it was only an aperitif. In those days of 1967–68 the MCC Secretariat could act almost without restraint in their work on behalf of the first-class game, provided the counties were kept informed. Negotiations with television, radio and cricket's one real venture into national sponsorship had always previously been conducted in the friendliest, most congenial and least commercially-minded manner possible. It had been desirable, naturally, to remain on good terms with the moguls of BBC TV and radio, with the Gillette company and the Post Office and anyone else who wished to be publicly associated with the great game, but was cricket being sold too cheaply? Players and professional administrators and staffs were badly paid, attendances were falling. At Lord's, Gubby Allen was talking of the possibility of leasing out part of the ground to Bertram Mills Circus. The catering rights for the whole of Lord's had just been sold on a twenty-one-year contract to Watney Mann for what may have looked a reasonable sum in 1967 . . . but a twenty-one-year contract with no review clauses and no built-in escalation of rent, and no share of the profit or of the turnover?

In general, an air of disenchantment was swirling round the game. Administrators and players each thought the other was to blame. However, urged on by the counties, Billy Griffith was prepared to let me make the running with a new, commercially-orientated approach. The first item on the agenda, and the only one capable of resolution in 1967, was the televising of the Gillette Cup, now in its fifth year. The BBC had been televising it (and indeed all other worthwhile cricket) with their widely acknowledged expertise from its inception, but they had been paying very little for the privilege. The recent enfranchisement of ITV stations provided a chance to create competition in the long term and to produce more money immediately. Misgivings abounded. We considered the seemliness of having Independent Television covering cricket, particularly the one-day variety, in the days before instant replays were possible with the resulting chance of important moments being lost in commercial breaks. Several meetings were held, with John Bromley and Jimmy Hill acting on behalf of London Weekend Television, and reassurance was at hand. Hill and Bromley had been quick to mention that they were both 'Bagenal men' – meaning that their agent was the Bagenal Harvey organization – but in the circumstances there seemed no reason why this should make any difference, even though relations between Billy Griffith and Bagenal Harvey had become somewhat strained. Nor, in terms of that first deal done with London Weekend TV, did it appear to make any odds at all.

To the chagrin of the BBC, a deal for the 1968 season was sealed. By the standards of those days the money was good, certainly better than the BBC had offered. We were reassured about the nature of the coverage. A letter was written on behalf of LWT expressing the thought that this was seen by Independent Television as a long-term project, and also recounting an understanding that the contract gave them a two-year option on coverage of the Gillette Cup. I wrote to say that if by 'option' it was meant that LWT would have every opportunity to bid for 1969 coverage, all things being equal, that was all right; but certainly we were in no position to grant an 'option'. If, I continued, there was any other expectation than the one I had outlined, please let me know. I received no reply to that letter.

On the day of the 1968 final, all went well until the climax. Warwickshire were closing fast on the Sussex total but the match was in the balance. As D. L. Bates ran in to bowl the

57th over, the clock stood at five minutes to seven. By 7 o'clock it was all over. Warwickshire had won by 4 wickets and the familiar scenes of jubilation rent the air at Lord's. Although I didn't know it at the time, these celebrations were not being shared by the audience at home. Nor had the desperately tense finish been shown. Indeed, not until after the advertisements, which came on bang on schedule, followed by the delights of the David Frost show for half an hour, was the result conveyed to a thoroughly irate audience.

The extent of the anguish was plain from the piles of post received at Lord's and, I daresay, by the representations made to LWT. (It never ceased to surprise me, incidentally, throughout my time at Lord's, how many people thought it was in our hands to control the vagaries of television production, right down to who should be commentating on a particular match.) Clearly some responsibility could be laid at our door, and there was a large element of bad luck involved, because the match, besides building to a tremendous climax had taken an unprecedentedly long time to finish. But it was not a happy augury.

The end of the season brought no respite. The d'Oliveira affair had been bubbling since August and showed few signs of subsiding; MCC had been hit where it hurt, and a special general meeting had been called to debate the issue in December. Before the 1969 season, no, before 1969 began, the televising of the Gillette Cup had to be sorted out. Also in the pipeline was the increasingly knotty problem of convincing the counties that the formation and organization of a new limited-overs Sunday competition would be in their best interests, certainly financially; and then finding a sponsor for it and, at the same time – or preferably before – interesting the television companies in covering it.

Some counties were sceptical about the Sunday league. There were those who, though undeniably short of cash, feared an adverse effect on membership. There were those who continued to support the concept of the Rothmans Cavaliers and BBC2 monopolizing Sunday afternoon cricket. Sections of the sporting press were increasingly savage in their criticisms of plans to introduce the competition in 1969. Michael Parkinson was one of those who seized the opportunity to give MCC a drubbing on virtually every subject including the move towards a Sunday league. These were times of living in a mental and moral minefield with no easy way out.

Throughout the summer of 1968 potential sponsors for the new competition had been approached. The field was wide, but by far the most attractive offer had been coaxed out of John Player, the tobacco company. We had explained our difficulties over obtaining television coverage: the independent channel could not guarantee continuous coverage, and the BBC appeared to be more than content with the Cavaliers. Further, various indicators – no more than straws in the wind, but there were quite a few of them – led to a growing belief that the Bagenal Harvey organization with its string of famous ex-cricketers, journalists and broadcasters, had the way blocked for TV coverage. And it seemed as if the same could be said even for some administrators, within the networks. I had been concerned when Jack Oaten of the BBC telephoned me to ask about the commercial channel's option on the Gillette Cup, as though he had been informed by someone somewhere that ITV had it all sewn up for 1969. Even after I had disabused him of the idea, the fact of his knowledge rankled.

Anyhow, the stumbling block had to be removed. First, I wrote a speech, an analysis of the whole situation for Billy Griffith to deliver to the counties at their next meeting. It was a call to the troops. For the future welfare of cricket, they were informed, it had been put forward that a Sunday competition organized and run on behalf of county cricket should begin in 1969. We could obtain a sponsor, a big one. What we had so far been unsuccessful in achieving was television coverage. It had to be made clear that county cricketers would not be taking part in televised cricket without the counties' permission and if they wanted a successful competition of their own, it meant denying permission to cricketers registered with them to take part in any rival competition on television. And that included the Cavaliers.

It was tough, but it was the only way to achieve a result in the short time available. My contacts at John Player had agreed that they would go ahead with sponsorship whether or not the league was televised, but for the long-term well-being of the venture television was an integral factor. The county game certainly could not afford the direct competition of its own players appearing in other televised games if the new league was to be successful.

All through the dying months of 1968, controversy danced around us. Letters, the press, the television and a stream of people, some of them in the cricketing firmament, and mostly connected with Bagenal Harvey or Rothmans, were soon descending in unfriendly fashion.

Nor were TV negotiations treading a primrose path. At last Peter Dimmock, head of BBC outside broadcasts, had put in a bid for the new John Player League but we were virtually sworn to secrecy in case anyone got to know of it. Linked adhesively in the BBC's proposals to cover the League every Sunday afternoon was coverage of the Gillette Cup. This presented no great problem on the face of it, but we felt bound to give ITV every chance to meet the more stringent conditions we were bound to impose after the 1968 fiasco with the Cup final; and felt honour-bound to give them every chance to continue into 1969 if everything else was equal. Besides, we were keen, if possible, to keep a foot in ITV's camp.

With Dimmock determinedly resisting all attempts to prise the BBC loose from a package deal, we were in effect saved from a difficult decision by ITV's inability to guarantee all we required in the way of coverage. The MCC solicitor, Alan Meyer, had confirmed that there was no option with ITV, and we felt we had explored every avenue with them as Billy Griffith had promised we would. A deal was struck with Dimmock, still in cloak-and-dagger circumstances in so far as meetings were taking place on neutral ground at slightly unlikely times. A two-year contract was signed. Coverage for the John Player League was assured. John Player had already been persuaded to part with £75,000 for a season's sponsorship. Now the BBC had secured coverage of the Gillette Cup and cricket was to benefit by a considerable addition to it finances.

Any relief felt at the outcome, any sense of achievement, any celebration that the dawn of a new day was with us, was short-lived, however.

No sooner had an announcement been made regarding the television contract, no sooner had E. W. Swanton in the *Daily Telegraph* congratulated Billy Griffith on a masterly piece of negotiation, than John Macmillan, head of sport for ITV, made an announcement of an entirely different kind. ITV and London Weekend were suing MCC for breach of contract and the break-ing of an undertaking. A writ had already arrived at Lord's. So now we were really in the soup. There never were and never had been such days. We had ventured a foot into the murky waters of commercialism and our toes had been severely nipped. As the main protagonist on our side, the man who had been behind negotiations with sponsors and TV throughout the long weary months, I was relatively calm. But the Law Courts beckoned and I had to admit to a fear of the unknown.

By now the Test and County Cricket Board had been formed and had to be kept abreast of the later stages of the nego-tiations. Indeed we had sought advice. The buck really stopped with Griffith and Bailey, but the Chairman of TCCB, Cecil Paris of Hampshire – one of the best servants cricket ever had and possibly the least well rewarded for all his endeavours – was the one named as the defendant in the hearing that took place in the High Court on Wednesday 12 February 1969.

The case lasted for three days and during the gruelling experi-ence for Billy and me on the one hand, and for Jimmy Hill and John Bromley on the other, a veritable galaxy of talent con-nected with the sporting world appeared among the onlookers. It seemed as though a three-line whip for Bagenal Harvey clients had been issued. Certainly Jimmy Hill and John Bromley did not lack support from the body of the court. Nor were they badly represented up front.

Leading for the plaintiffs was Geoffrey Howe QC, then just a Member of Parliament; now, of course, Foreign Secretary. His junior, whose eloquence and style when conducting the case in the absence of his leading counsel drew praise from Mr Justice Megaw, was Robert Alexander. We were to meet later as adversaries in another case when he had become a QC, a leading counsel in his own right, and he was appearing on behalf of an enterprise at whose head stood someone unknown to us in 1969 – one Kerry Packer.

In the case involving ITV we were represented by Michael Kempster. He was a distinguished junior counsel and, in spite of the bewildered air of his clients, he brought us home at the gallop. MCC and TCCB were completely vindicated. It was Michael Kempster QC who led for ICC and TCCB in the case later to be brought by Packer. But that, as they say, is another story.

I was told shortly after the case that Peter Dimmock's action in entering into a package deal for the John Player League and Gillette Cup had come as both a surprise and a shock to Bagenal Harvey and that Bagenal had shown his considerable surprise and displeasure when the facts came out in court. It was not quite the end of the Cavaliers. They continued playing during the 1969 season, but without television coverage the cause was doomed. It was necessarily so but it gave me no great satisfaction.

Had all the vituperations engendered through press and television against the counties' own competition been worth it? The answer was not long in arriving. On the first Sunday at Lord's, more than twice the usual Sunday paying crowd turned up to see Middlesex. Over the weeks, the advertising campaign by John Player took hold, and as the reality of the cricket, in contrast to the somewhat contrived formula of the Cavaliers' game, endeared itself to the *aficionados*, there was no doubt that we had a financial success on our hands.

Despite its shortcomings from the point of view of the traditionalists, the John Player League was probably the greatest single breakthrough made in those turbulent years. It pointed the way to relative prosperity and it also introduced an urgency which rubbed off on other forms of cricket. The short runs taken, the diving about in the field, the sixes and fours were electrifying. A new dimension to the skills of county cricketers was recognized. This, together with the chance of seeing the beginning and the end of an exciting match played by the best players in England, introduced a new type of spectator to county grounds. Watching cricket became an occasion for the whole family.

Of course, promotion on television was an essential part of all this. Not only did the games reach a large audience, but with a guarantee of TV coverage at least once a year even the lowliest county club could think in terms of making money from ground advertising, quite apart from the extra money the sponsors were prepared to pay for this facility.

At the beginning of 1969 it had been decided that a sub-committee of the new Test and County Cricket Board should be formed to deal with public relations and promotions on behalf of the game. It was a logical step. It meant that Billy Griffith and I would no longer be ploughing a lonely furrow. But I viewed with mixed feelings the prospect of being stuck in the middle between the somewhat gentlemanly unbusinesslike approach of MCC through Billy Griffith, and the go-ahead methods of a group of wheeler-dealers and whiz-kids.

The sub-committee, chaired by Raman Subba Row, were out to prove themselves. I began to hear phrases like 'modern marketing techniques' echoing round the Committee Room at Lord's (you didn't often hear these expressions in connection with cricket in those days). It was also agreed that I should have assistance with what had become an enormous workload for one person. Thus began a fruitful partnership with Ron Roe who was appointed promotions officer for TCCB.

Once it has been established that the MCC Secretariat should carry out the business of the sub-committee and that nobody else on the sub-committee was involved in that side of things, we settled down to do some useful work.

It was quickly established with the counties that if we were to win we had to be prepared to lose. The negotiations with the BBC over the forthcoming series, England v. West Indies, had not yet begun although there were only ten weeks to go before the start of the season. The counties were asked whether they would be prepared to back a new stance. Would they be prepared to go without TV for Test matches in 1969 if we could not get what we considered a satisfactory deal? Somewhat rashly perhaps the counties agreed. We had a free hand – at least on paper – although I knew that nobody would thank us if we got it wrong.

In Peter Dimmock the BBC had a tried, proven and tough negotiator. He had the ability to seize the initiative and retain it. It was our job not to let this happen. We decided to start the bidding rather than, as in past years, wait for him to tell us how much the BBC could afford.

I did not, by any means, know all the answers and the others knew no more; but having perused the TV ratings for Test matches, which had not been done by our predecessors, having measured these against other programmes, having discovered what the BBC were paying for other outside broadcasts, having assessed the potential of the West Indies tour as opposed to others, and having taken into account various factors such as inflation since the last four-year contract had been drawn up in 1964, it was agreed that I should write a letter. We aimed high. We explained why we had aimed high. In fact we asked for three times the amount previously paid by the BBC for each year of a four-year contract and we asked it for a one-year contract, for 1969 only. It was explained that we were trying to establish a proper base for the televising of Test matches, which the Committee believed had been undersold to an extraordinary degree in the past.

Naturally the BBC did not concur. Exchanges of correspondence were reported back to the sub-committee, meetings with Peter Dimmock and others on the BBC side took place. We did not budge and time galloped along. The BBC tried all routes, reverting to backdoor tactics through Billy Griffith and members of the MCC hierarchy whom we managed to persuade not to interfere, but to leave matters in our hands. We knew what we were doing, we said . . . with fingers crossed.

By this time I knew I was in a vulnerable position. I was the negotiator and my neck was on the block. The sub-committee were behind me every step of the way, but there would be no great thanks from anyone, least of all from those who had been responsible under the old regime, if Test cricket was not televised in 1969. Negotiations continued. The court case with London Weekend Television came and went. We did a deal to get the John Player League matches featured on TV. We employed the services of Hobson Bates, a friendly advertising agency, to help with various promotional aspects of the game. The West Indies team arrived on 21 April. Still there was no Test match television contract.

It was May, with the first Test due on 12 June, before the first cracks began to appear in the BBC edifice. The *Radio Times* was shortly due to go to press for the week in which the Test began, I was informed. Were we prepared to reconsider, or should the Test matches not be part of the *Radio Times* copy? It was clear that a deadline was fast approaching. I replied that I would of course be prepared to talk, but there was no point unless the BBC were prepared to see our point of view.

The matter had to be cleared by 24 May, Whit weekend. It was nail-biting time. It was a psychologically vital point that the BBC should make the first approach to set up a meeting, and I thought Peter Dimmock would resist it. If this was to be accomplished in time for inclusion in the *Radio Times*, Thursday 22 May was the crucial day for a meeting to be fixed. From 5 p.m. onwards I sat at my desk willing my fingers not to stray towards the telephone. Did it matter who rang whom? At 5.28 my phone rang. BBC were on the line. We had done it. We had been prepared to settle for half of what we had originally demanded. We emerged with two-thirds for a two-year contract, and twice as much as before for a Test series in a four-year contract.

There was nothing particularly clever in what had been achieved. But the story illustrates how far we were prepared to go to get substantially more money into the game. Each new project was assessed realistically. Immense pains were taken to see that the cricket authorities remained in charge of the cricket and that we sold ourselves dearly but fairly.

During the next five years income from sources old and new was greatly increased. The new included the Benson and Hedges Cup, dreamed up by me as an early-season combination of league and knock-out cricket, which would still permit twenty or more championship games in a season, then considered essential; and the Prudential Trophy matches – the beginning of the one-day internationals, later adopted throughout the international scene and then seized upon avidly by Kerry Packer. These in turn gave rise to the Prudential World Cup. For all these sponsorship deals we were blessed by the pleasantest possible people to deal with, who understood that we would do everything in our power to promote their names through the media and on the grounds where their competitions were played, but that all other arrangements were in the hands of the individual clubs. And the cricket format was in the hands of the cricket authorities. It all worked remarkably well.

Thus through the late 1960s and early 1970s we danced and weaved our way. A cricket magazine commissioned and edited on behalf of TCCB; the Test match telephone service; first-day covers; new radio contracts negotiated, as with TV, along proper commercial lines. The TCCB sub-committee were a formidable lot to have at one's back, and God knows we were only a part of cricket's overall resurgence.

Helped by the introduction of top-class overseas players into the domestic scene, the county players – now better paid – took on a new lease of life. With four competitions, all but the county championship being sponsored, each county felt there was a chance of winning something. The days of monopoly by a relatively select number of counties, such as Yorkshire, Surrey or Middlesex, gradually disappeared. Indeed Yorkshire, by their admirably consistent adherence to the policy which allowed only those born in Yorkshire to play for the county, were to embark upon a long road of exceptional failure as the likes of Somerset, Essex and Leicestershire made the most of the opportunities presented by the new dispensation and the freedom of action springing from a reliable flow of cash from central sources.

At the same time, stage by stage, the need to adapt to the one-day game saw a revival of some of the old, exciting skills which spilled over into the three-day game and, indeed, into Test match cricket. The fielding improved – bad fielders were tolerated less and less. Running between the wickets gained a new and vital urgency. In most cases occupation of the crease was overtaken by enterprising batsmanship. The effect was felt universally. A revival of the game in England slowly gathered an irresistible momentum. That all this was being presented admirably on BBC television meant the widest possible audience.

There were bound to be side effects and a number of these can be seen in the game today. The advent of overseas players, especially of ready made fast bowlers, has had its effect on the outlook of counties who have found it easier to buy overseas than train aspiring youngsters in their own back yard. This has done nothing for the reservoir of talent available to the England selectors. The disciplines of the one-day game in English domestic cricket are often blamed for the wayward techniques of English batsmen. Doubtless there is an element of truth in this.

Yet who, when faced with the malnutrition of the 1960s, would have opted for the undernourished, often neglected child that English cricket was then? The robust youth that we have today presents his problems but at least he is active and flourishing.

The selling of the new game, the injection of a fresh approach and an eye to the way the game has been presented, have been factors in what I would see as a considerable success story. The importance of those early days of the TCCB, prompted by Raman Subba Row and his sub-committee, cannot be over-estimated. The organizational elements of this work, undertaken by other members of the MCC/TCCB Secretariat (notably Donald Carr), and by the numerous sub-committees involved, were just as important, if less glamorous. On the whole, we had worked well as a team and cricket had been well served.

3

SOUTH AFRICA IS ALWAYS
WITH US

DIRECT INVOLVEMENT IN the political aspects of cricket and
South Africa began for me when I joined the MCC in
1967 and continued right through my career at Lord's. Like the
poor it was always with us and, as with the poor, however
hard we tried we could do precious little to improve the position.

In those early days the Labour government of Harold Wilson
was in power. For the first time we had a Minister for Sport.
His powers were strictly limited under the law of the land but,
as is often the case with socialist regimes, this did nothing to
prevent interference of a direct kind in the affairs of various
sporting bodies, in so far as they would allow it. Denis Howell
had been quick to take an interest in cricket, both as to the way
it was being governed and by whom, and the position *vis-à-vis*
England playing against South Africa; or, as his government
would prefer, not playing.

The story of Basil d'Oliveira is well known; too well known

for much background detail to be necessary. It is, however, important to recognize that South Africa, as represented by the South African Cricket Association, was in 1968 an important senior member of the international cricket fraternity. It was a founder member of the International Cricket Conference with MCC and Australia, and arguably the foremost cricket nation in the world at international level. The cricket world was strongly inclined towards getting on with the game with South Africa – or anybody else – leaving politics to the politicians. It was, and always will be, an attitude of substance, if your brief is the administration of your sport and the well-being of your sport and your penchant is loyalty to good, time-honoured and trusted friends, and if you believe that contact is more productive than isolation. If politics were to be an issue when opponents in sport were under consideration, there were, even then, a number of countries who might be left out of the reckoning.

Equally, it was naïve in the extreme to suppose that the sub-ject of South Africa as it presented itself in the late 1960s, with all its racial overtones, was not something abnormal, especially with the population of Britain as mixed as it had now become, and with all the elasticity that moral rather than legal arguments contain.

What brought the issue of cricket against South Africa into searching, unwavering focus was the presence in the English ranks during the 1967–68 tour of the West Indies, and then in the first Test of the summer of 1968 against Australia, of one Basil d'Oliveira, a fine and gutsy all-rounder, who was also a Cape Coloured and qualified to play for England by virtue, at least partly, of the fact that the laws of his own country made it impossible for him to play for South Africa. MCC was aware that everything possible should be done to clarify what would happen if d'Oliveira were picked to represent them on a tour of South Africa, scheduled to take place in the English winter of 1968–69.

The advice of Denis Howell, the Minister for Sport, had been to write to the South African Cricket Association seeking assurance that whoever was picked would be welcomed to their shores. Given the nature of the South African Nationalist government's views and the framing of the question, it was hardly surprising that no answer was forthcoming.

The advice of Sir Alec Douglas Home to the MCC Committee was not to press for an answer but to select the team on merit. No government (for it was without question that the South African government would be responsible) would answer a hypothetical question of the kind posed by our letter. It was the only possible way to deal with the matter, short of cancelling the tour because no answer had been received. MCC was in the business of protecting tours and fostering cricket, not cancelling tours.

It left Doug Insole and his fellow selectors with a task which, short of a series of performances by d'Oliveira which could make the selection a crystal-clear formality one way or the other, would always leave the selection process open to doubt. The prime question was: in such a climate, could justice be done and be seen to be done?

Basil d'Oliveira played in two Test matches that summer – the first and the last. In the first at Old Trafford he made 87 not out, out of a total of 253. He was left out of the team for the second at Lord's because, according to an explanation given later by Colin Cowdrey, his bowling had not come up to scratch at Manchester.

My own role, with so much going on, was confusing. I had no part in the thinking processes which led to the selectors' decisions, nor was I privy to the reasons behind them. Yet the shoals of letters that landed at Lord's made their way to my desk and had to be dealt with.

The political manoeuvrings alleged to be going on behind the scenes – d'Oliveira being importuned in a lay-by and promised huge rewards by the head of a South African commercial enterprise if he would make himself unavailable for the **South Africa tour; a letter to the Secretary of MCC from** a Committee member, saying that Lord (Charles) Cobham had been told by the South African Prime Minister, Mr Vorster, that d'Oliveira would never be allowed into South Africa as a member of the MCC team – were known to me. But wiser heads than mine were dealing with problems of that nature, if indeed there was any substance in them.

Certain it was that d'Oliveira was under microscopic scrutiny throughout that summer. His batting and bowling performances were assessed, and then his selection and non-selection rationalized by those responsible, to a degree which argued either great conscientiousness or self-deception. I'm sure it was the former, but it was easy to see that the other interpretation could have presented itself to many.

I know something about the game, but I was willing to accept that the boys who played at Test level and had done so with distinction for many years knew a great deal more about it than I, and I was unquestioning in my confidence that there were good cricketing reasons for everything that was done. But when you look back on the sequence of events and the reasons given for the erratic path they followed, there has to be some sympathy for the ordinary cricket follower. The sceptic had a field-day at the time, and small wonder.

As explained by Cowdrey later, d'Oliveira was dropped from the second Test at Lord's, having 'batted splendidly for 87 not out', because a 'seam bowler' rather than a 'swing bowler' was required at Lord's. He was replaced by Barry Knight who acquitted himself well with the ball.

Comes the fifth Test match, and Cowdrey is impressed by the fact that during a match between Kent and Surrey at The Oval, the medium-pacers were causing the problems on a pitch 'only eight yards away from the Test match pitch'. So the Kent and England captain was minded to have a medium-pacer up his sleeve in case any of the bowlers selected should cry off. On this occasion it did not much matter, apparently, whether it was a swing or seam bowler, because Knight, who had replaced d'Oliveira at Lord's, was first in line after Tom Cartwright, while d'Oliveira came third in the line of replacements. Knight and Cartwright, though both had been playing in county matches at the time of asking, were ruled out through lack of fitness, neither, as Cowdrey later related, being fit enough to play in a Test match. Cowdrey took it upon himself to call up d'Oliveira for the Oval Test as one of the twelve from whom the team was to be picked.

Pausing for breath for a moment, the sequence of events can be summarized as follows. Essentially a batsman who bowls, d'Oliveira, is dropped for the second Test match because his bowling is medium-paced and relies primarily on swing, although his batting has been excellent. Despite a string of low scores in county matches, he is recalled for the fifth Test because he is also a medium-pace swing bowler, although his style is different from either of those who were chosen in front of him but in the event could not play. Now read on . . .

The England team as originally picked already had five front-line bowlers: Snow, Brown, Higgs, Illingworth and Underwood. Despite this well-balanced attack, d'Oliveira is called up to join the twelve; Roger Prideaux cries off on the day before the match. Prideaux is an opening batsman. Yet d'Oliveira is drafted into the team to replace him. Somebody 'up there' must have had a hand in this mysterious selection process. And somebody 'up there' must have been watching as England's sixth bowler, batting at no. 5, scored 158 runs and laid the foundation for a victory over Australia to square the series. His contribution with the ball was negligible.

I was at The Oval on the final day, had seen the England victory and had taken part in the wave of speculation which followed Basil d'Oliveira's innings. One elder statesman of the game had been full of the sheer luck of Dolly's performance. Dropped on 31 he had been, but I had missed the other two chances attributed to him by the gentleman who had spoken to me.

My thoughts were primarily selfish. How could we possibly cope with the press and the public if Dolly wasn't picked? Yet,

I told myself, the selectors are bound to follow understandable cricketing principles and when all things are considered they can't possibly leave out the man who has just scored 158 against Australia. Moreover, although public opinion was rarely considered in those days, it must surely now play its part. It would be bad if the South African government prevented the tour, but far worse if MCC were left to explain the almost inexplicable.

After the match, Colin Cowdrey was kind enough to offer me a lift to Lord's where he would be attending the meeting of the selectors that evening. I climbed into MCC 307, the captain's Jaguar, and virtually his first words, in reply to my congratulatory offering, were: 'Thanks. It's good to have beaten the Aussies. It looks as though we shall have problems with South Africa, though. They can't leave Basil out of the team. Not now.'

Thinking I knew the powers of the captain when it came to the selection process, whether he was Colin Cowdrey or anyone else, I prepared myself overnight for the need to handle whatever reaction might come from South Africa after the announcement of the team which was due the following morning. When I arrived at Lord's early the next day, Billy Griffith and Donald Carr were clearly not quite themselves as I met them in the Committee Room. Both had been present at the Selection Committee meeting, together with the England captain, Gubby Allen, Arthur Gilligan, Leslie Ames and the selectors: Doug Insole, in the chair, Peter May, Don Kenyon and Alec Bedser.

There was a nervous uncertain air about the place. I was told that d'Oliveira was not in the party of sixteen.

Two hours later the press conference was hushed as Doug Insole announced the team. When the name of d'Oliveira went unmentioned the hush was different. This was of the deathly kind. Some kind of bet between Ian Wooldridge of the *Daily Mail* and Clive Taylor of the *Sun* was settled on the spot. Questions were asked. Doug Insole explained the selectors' thinking. Essentially, it had been a question of balance and the type of wickets now being produced in South Africa. The team had been selected entirely on merit. Yes, d'Oliveira was unlucky not to be going. But then the selectors would have liked to be taking Colin Milburn, among others. The conclusion had been that Cartwright would be a key figure on the tour with his medium-pace bowling. There simply was not room for Basil d'Oliveira.

It did not go unnoticed how much of a key figure Tom Cartwright had become without taking part in a single Test match that summer. His unavailability for the Oval Test had been responsible for Basil's chance, which had been grasped with both hands. Now he was seen as the man who was to be preferred. There *was* a logic about it all, but would anyone understand?

The answer was that not too many people did. Lord's was snowed under with mail – 70 per cent critical, 20 per cent understanding, the balance supportive from a racist point of view – and it was difficult to know which way to turn. A particular telegram sent to Doug Insole raised a wan smile at the time. It went something like this: 'Congratulations on a selection that will have the support of all right-minded people. I, and millions of others, applaud your decision'. It was signed: ADOLF HITLER.

Just what would have happened if the tour had taken place with the team selected will never be known. Probably life would have been even more difficult, if that were possible, than it had already become. As I went about my business, determinedly putting the best face on every answer to every question, accompanying Doug Insole and others to explanatory interviews on television, writing explanatory articles without apparently achieving very much, I was forcibly reminded that I had taken on not so much a job as a way of life.

Meetings were taking place thick and fast. The routine jobs did not diminish. Home was where you could find it when you could remember where it was.

Then, just as the storm seemed to be subsiding, Tom Cartwright, the bowler picked for his special ability to perform on the wickets thought to be produced currently in South Africa, cried off. As everyone knows, d'Oliveira was chosen to replace him.

It was extraordinary how often Dolly had been called up, apparently partly as, or to replace, a bowler, when his quality performances in Tests that season had been as a batsman. The rationale may have been baffling, but at least the sheer weight of the problem had now been lifted from the shoulders of the chairman of selectors, who was facing most of the criticism, and from MCC, where Billy Griffith and I were in the front line and for whom a sensible quality of life had become impossible. Mr Vorster, the South African Prime Minister of the time, then made the move which, more than any other, has led to the virtual exclusion of South Africa as a force in representative international sport. He pronounced that the inclusion of d'Oliveira in the MCC team was politically motivated; a deliberate provocation. South Africa could not accept d'Oliveira in such circumstances. Unfortunately, the timing and nature of events surrounding Dolly's selection gave the South African Prime Minister a perfect opportunity to lay the blame fair and square at the door of English cricket.

For all the anguish at the thought of all our cricketing friends in South Africa being victims of the South African government's policies – with which they disagreed wholeheartedly – there was nothing more to be done but cancel the tour.

I was surprised to read in the press, almost before Vorster's speech had sunk in, that Colin Cowdrey was talking of flying out to South Africa to make Mr Vorster see the light. Apparently the idea was to explain to Vorster how all decisions had been made on cricketing grounds. Even with my limited experience of these things, it seemed to be the time to forget the gratuitous public relations and say something simple and straightforward. I was fortunate enough to have just such a chance when Billy Griffith suggested I go on television, in answer to an invitation by ITN, to clarify the position.

During a live interview with dear old Reggie Bosanquet, then at the top of his form as a TV presenter, I was able to make some sort of fist of it. 'Is it true that, even at this late stage, MCC are trying everything to save the tour?' he asked.

'I can see no possibility of that,' I said.

'Colin Cowdrey is apparently thinking of flying to South Africa to sort things out,' he went on. 'Surely this indicates that the cricket authorities are trying to save the tour?'

'I think Colin is expressing views which are entirely his own', I replied, feeling (concerned as I was at the need to contradict Colin) that it was time the matter was put into proper perspective. 'The tour to South Africa is beyond recall, as I see it.'

And so it was. Nothing official had been decided, but it was ludicrous to suppose there was a chance of any different outcome. Jack Cheetham and Arthur Coy, President and Vice-president of the South African Cricket Association, came to London and met the MCC Committee at Lord's. They returned with all our sympathy but otherwise empty handed. It was realized that the matter had been taken out of the hands of cricketers in South Africa. There could be no tour. It was time to regroup and start again; consideration, long and hard, had to be given to that.

There was plenty to think about, an enormous amount to do. South Africa were due to tour England in 1970. Then there was the formation of the new Cricket Council, and the Test and County Cricket Board and the parlous state of domestic cricket, and a special meeting of MCC on the whole South African issue, called by David Sheppard, Mike Brearley and others, not to mention the problems caused by ITV's coverage of the Gillette Cup final and the need simply to get on with the common task, the daily round.

On the South African front the MCC Committee were faced immediately with a Special General Meeting on the whole emotive issue of playing cricket against South Africa. Nothing is more debilitating than when friends fall out and your job, whatever your convictions, is in a sense to hold the ring.

In assessing the whole ghastly problem it was necessary, in those days, when the issue of sport and South Africa was at the teething stage, to ask oneself what cricket administration should be setting out to achieve. At that time the phrase best able to express MCC's motivation, and one which the Club had lived up to exceedingly well throughout the years, was 'to foster cricket wherever it is played'. Matters concerning politicians were also the concern of us all, but the playing of cricket was not or *should* not be the concern of politicians unless legislation demanded that it should be so. Moral issues were for individuals and these beliefs should be respected; but in those days the argument for retaining contact through the game, linked with an old-fashioned notion of not letting down those in South Africa who had contributed so much to the game internationally, were principles to which the majority adhered.

It was understood that those who nourished cricket in South Africa were in the grip of a government whose laws were anathema to most who thought about it at all, and that included those who played and administered cricket there. They had fought side by side with England during the war. Now they needed our help and support. We should lend it to them.

I have described the views of the majority within the cricket world in 1968 as nearly as I can. They are views which persist though, rightly or wrongly, they are given much less credence today. Events have overtaken them.

Church House, Westminster, on 5 December 1968, presented a scene which in many ways showed MCC at its best. A wide range of opinion was voiced in a number of sensible, lucid speeches from both sides. An unmistakable undercurrent of passion and conviction pervaded the hall, yet the whole meeting was conducted in a civilized, unpersonalized way. It was the last and perhaps the most important single international issue decided by MCC, before such matters became the province of the newly formed Cricket Council. With the help of that formidable weapon, the postal vote, MCC members made it clear that South Africa should remain on the agenda for future consideration. Everyone agreed that Basil d'Oliveira had emerged the untarnished hero of the hour. On most other things they agreed to differ.

There was no doubt, however, that the d'Oliveira affair had dealt poor old MCC a grievous wound. David Sheppard had shown himself to be a persuasive exponent of the 'no cricket with South Africa until apartheid is abolished' school of thought. As a former England captain and a man of the church he was to prove a formidable opponent when it came to laying plans for the 1970 South African tour of England. And, Peter Hain, a South African student then at London University, and an outspoken critic of South Africa, was soon to make his presence felt.

Although the whole question of to play or not to play now came within the province of the Cricket Council through the Test and County Cricket Board, operations at the decision-making and executive levels were much the same as they had been when MCC ruled the roost officially.

Once a decision had been made to go ahead with the 1970 tour, Lord's knew what it was like to be in a state of siege. With Raman Subba Row as a consultant, employed by MCC at my request to lend a hand with the immense task of putting the best possible public face on cricket's cause, we worked night and day at myriad tasks and at many levels. These ranged from government to public: from Home Secretary to back-benchers; from Archbishop of Canterbury, through a company of Bishops and the Reverend David Sheppard to the humblest curate in the land; from Commissioners of Police, through Special Branch to the local constabulary; from newspaper editors to lowly hacks; from chairmen of companies with connections with South Africa to the widow with her mite who was prepared to contribute to the cause.

They were exciting and sometimes intensely rewarding times; occasionally almost heart-breaking. We were fighting for the world of cricket as we knew it; for the right to play cricket under the law of the land. There was nothing but discouragement from Harold Wilson's Labour government, but a vast wave of encouragement from the cricket-loving public, and all the time there was the feeling that here was something worth fighting for, even if defined as vaguely as freedom under the law. The issues were difficult to define simply. The emotions tended always to cloud the facts. It is possibly fair to say that the Cricket Council, now the governing body for all cricket in the UK, were intent on giving their friends and opposite numbers in South Africa the opportunity to show, by their conduct in what was bound to be a strife-ridden series, that they were part of a cricketing community which transcended other factors when it came to cricket. The actions of the South African government should not be ascribed to South African cricketers. The Cricket Council had ascertained, through every available channel, that the playing of cricket in England was a legal pursuit. The tour, according to the opinion polls, was supported by the vast majority of ordinary people in Britain.

Against this it was argued – and argued chiefly by those who were doing all in their power to encourage disruption of the tour by means ranging through a wide spectrum – that the tour would be interpreted as showing support for apartheid, that it would be bad for community relations in Britain, and that it would have severe implications for the forces of law and order. In this connection we were continually assured, by the appropriate government departments, that the forces of law and order would be well able to cope. In the year of a general election they could scarcely say otherwise. And then there was the effect of the tour on other sporting events. In those comparatively straightforward days, we could not see that that was our responsibility.

As the scenario unfolded, it became clear to us that if the tour were to be called off then the government would have to do it. Otherwise, we should press on. The rule of a minority, no matter how well-intentioned, had not become part of the British way of life. It should be for the government to decide whether a tour could be sustained in the face of that minority. As far as cricket was concerned the Cricket Council had made its decision and the English counties and their players were behind them.

Following the announcement of the proposed itinerary in September 1969, Peter Hain formed the Stop the Seventy Tour committee. He had been involved in disrupting a match between Oxford University and a private team from South Africa the previous summer. He was only nineteen years of age, but extraordinarily articulate. Well advised legally, his 'non-violent' campaign enabled him to capture the headlines and the TV interviews, and quickly to assume the role of spokesman for – to use his own words – 'the young people of this country'.

He and his followers, by one of those extraordinary quirks of fate, were given the opportunity to cut their teeth and perfect their 'non-violent' techniques of disruption on the South African rugby tour of Britain which took place during the winter of 1969–70. Of course the movement attracted the violent, who seized the perfect opportunity to back an organization which had the implied, if not the overt, support of the British government.

Jack Cheetham and Arthur Coy of the South African Cricket Association were in London for talks in November 1969 and confirmed that the South African team would be chosen entirely on merit. Unfortunately, while this was undoubtedly true, it had to be accepted that there were no coloured or black cricketers anywhere near the required standard.

I accompanied both men to Twickenham for the England v. South Africa match. The police ringed the touch-line and faced the crowd, not the play. They were magnificent. I was particularly impressed by the demeanour of one black policeman, who was plainly disgusted by the antics of the demonstrators in front of him and the obscenities being hurled his way. Nonetheless, he remained stoically calm throughout, still facing the crowd as the last whistle blew.

Cheetham and Coy watched it all and showed no misgivings about the forthcoming tour. There was little doubt in my mind, however, that unless things took a drastic turn for the better, the itinerary for the summer of 1970 would have to be truncated. Only Test match grounds would be capable of being defended – and six hours' play would make much greater demands than ninety minutes at Twickenham.

The next six months or so passed in a blur of activity of varying scope but all working towards a common end. Raman Subba Row and I distributed pamphlets outside the gates at Twickenham enlisting support for saving the tour among an ostensibly sympathetic crowd, but we met with limited success because people thought we were connected with the opposite faction, and there was little time to explain that we were not.

A meeting of the Cricket Council at Lord's on 27 November 1969 confirmed that the tour would go ahead after possible costs to cricket of maintaining law and order had been calculated and fresh approaches to the counties and the Home Office instigated. Further confirmation of the tour came at a TCCB meeting on 10 and 11 December at which Gubby Allen emerged not only as a strong champion but also as a persuasive advocate of the cause. During the meeting I drafted, with Raman Subba Row, the following statement:

> The Test and County Cricket Board, comprising representatives from all first-class counties and the minor counties, have confirmed unanimously that the South African tour will take place.
>
> In reaffirming their decision, they repeat their aversion to racial discrimination of any kind. They also respect the rights of those who wish to demonstrate peacefully.
>
> Equally they are unanimous in their resolve to uphold the rights of individuals in this country to take part in lawful pursuits, particularly where these pursuits have the support of the majority.

The BBC televised live a debate on the whole subject. Among those appearing for the Cricket Council were MCC's President, the delightful Maurice Allom, Billy Griffith, and Sir Peter Rawlinson, later a Conservative Attorney-General. On the other side were the combined talents of David Sheppard, Peter Hain and Brian Walden, then a junior minister in the Labour government. It was riveting stuff. I was so embroiled that I failed to acknowledge David Sheppard during refreshments before the programme, but agreed with him that we should remain good friends even though we were temporarily on opposite sides. The programme gave me a feeling of quiet triumph (there wasn't too much triumph about at that time) after Rawlinson had demolished Hain on the question of what was and was not permissible in the way of 'peaceful demonstration'.

The heart-searching went on continually behind the scenes over costs, over danger, over the long-term future of the game. The decision in the end was to carry on; though during January 1970, Billy Griffith showed increasing signs of stress and illness and retired hurt for a week or two. Before that, signs had been discovered of a naïve attempt to start a fire at Lord's during the watches of the night, and several other grounds had been the subject of attack during the night of 19 January.

With Gubby Allen, I visited Quintin Hogg (previously and later Lord Hailsham), then in opposition and practising as a barrister. We explained our worries and fears on the law and order issue and he drafted a substantial memorandum to be sent to the Home Office.

After this had been approved by the Council and sent off, only a few weeks elapsed before we were asked to attend upon Jim Callaghan, the Home Secretary, at his office in Whitehall. By then the tour had been reduced to twelve matches, we had enlisted the help of a professional fund-raiser and several MCC members who were also financial moguls in the City, and were well on the way to establishing what later became known as the Save the Seventy Tour fund. It was a determined bunch who went to meet Mr Callaghan and I believe he was somewhat surprised at just how resolute we were. Urbanely and skilfully he pointed out the various ways in which disruption could be caused, he pointed to the noise, the shining of mirrors, and other diabolical tricks at the disposal of the protesters. We listened courteously, made a few points of our own, and then asked if we could be assured that the forces of law and order could deal with what came along. He assured us they could. I suppose there was little else, politically, that he could say.

None of this in any way diminished the support given to the Stop the Seventy Tour movement by government sources. Harold Wilson, in a broadcast on BBC TV full of innuendo, told the nation on 16 April to 'feel free to demonstrate' at any of the matches. 'The Cricket Council,' he said, 'should not feel they are being subjected to blackmail, but . . .' It was pressure about as subtle as a sledgehammer; an open invitation to disrupt the tour.

That broadcast provoked a sharp response on behalf of the Cricket Council. Throughout the Hain campaign our public statements and press releases had been to the point, but impeccably restrained. We had been respectful without being subservient, even in the face of provocation. But this broadcast by the Prime Minister on David Coleman's *Sportsnight* wasn't just another go at the cricket authorities by the BBC. It was much more serious, critical even. The press rang my office and they rang again and rang again. I said we would make a statement as soon as possible.

Very late that evening I was sitting in my office attempting to draft some sort of statement as a riposte when Raman Subba Row came on the phone. He, too, had been thinking that an immediate reply to Wilson's broadcast was essential. Together, over the telephone, we worked out a short statement. He convinced me that it should be released whether or not I was able to contact the Chairman or the Secretary of the Cricket Council. I called Billy Griffith several times and tried to reach the Chairman. No luck. I learned later that poor Billy had taken his telephone off the hook in order to get some sleep.

Finally, I rang the Press Association and gave out a statement which went something like this:

'In his broadcast this evening, the Prime Minister referred to the right of all people to demonstrate freely during cricket matches against the South Africans this summer. He also mentioned that the Cricket Council should not feel that they were being blackmailed.

It is for the Prime Minister to decide whether incitement to demonstrate constitutes blackmail, just as it is for the government to decide whether law and order can be maintained in the face of public demonstrations.

If for these or any other reasons the Prime Minister feels that the tour by the South Africans should not go ahead, then he should come out and say so, to the South African government.'

There was consternation in the camp the following morning. Concern was expressed at the tone as well as the lack of authorization of the statement. It fact it appeared to have struck just the right spot. The reaction among supporters was enthusiastic. There was complete silence from government sources.

The days before the tour were fast sinking in number. On 23 April, St George's day, the 1970 Tour Fund was launched by Charles Newman VC, a great man and hero of the St Nazaire raid, and ideally suited to the purpose. The fund declared two aims: to help finance the tour, yes; but also to further the objectives of multi-racial cricket in South Africa. It was to prove a success, well in line with our highest hopes.

The largest single contribution was for £3,000. It came from Geoffrey Poore, the man who had headed BSA when it was a flourishing business and BSA was the name you thought of when someone mentioned motor-bikes. With the cheque was a letter, written along the following lines: 'I enclose this cheque in the knowledge that the cricket authorities, with the best of motives, have landed themselves in a lot of trouble, first with d'Oliveira and now because they quite rightly insist on going ahead with cricket against South Africa. I hope my donation will serve to bail you out, if only to buy a few miles of barbed wire.'

And barbed wire there was, at Lord's and elsewhere. What with spotlights trained on the playing area as soon as dusk fell and barbed wire round the square, we were back to wartime with a vengeance.

On the political front we were involved in what has now become an almost commonplace tactic, but in those days was unheard of. We had a meeting with Alastair Ross, chairman of the Commonwealth Games Committee. The black nations of Africa – at least thirteen of them – had threatened to withdraw from the games unless the tour was called off. We did not want this to happen, of course, but politely yet firmly we had to make it clear that cricket was our chief concern and some other solution should be found. The politicians who controlled the athletes should be made aware that such tactics were not consistent with the proper running of any sport. Otherwise complete anarchy would prevail. During the early summer of 1970, I met more politicians in a couple of months than in a normal lifetime for a cricket administrator. Desmond Donnelly, Ted Heath, Edward Boyle, John Biggs-Davison, Jim Callaghan, Quintin Hogg, Denis Howell were among them. The list wasn't endless but it seemed so. During the same period we met various people expressing concern at the affect of the tour on community relations. We met Sir Edward Boyle, David Sheppard and others from the Campaign for Fair Cricket. We also met representatives from the Race Relations Board.

On 18 May the impossible was accomplished when we managed to hold a meeting at Lord's of the full Cricket Council without anyone else knowing. In peace and quiet the whole position was discussed and analysed. Afterwards Raman and I drafted a statement, about a thousand words long, which was approved by those appointed by the Council to do so. It dealt with all the matters raised over the years and months, it expressed an understanding of the point of view of others on a wide range of subjects. It delineated what the Council felt to be its own responsibility and that of the government. It pointed out that 'No further Test tours will take place between South

Africa and this country until such time as Test cricket is played and tours are selected on a multi-racial basis in South Africa'.

The Council confirmed that they had re-assessed their responsibilities and felt these to relate to:

1. Cricket and cricketers in the UK and throughout the world
2. The other sports and sportsmen

But the vital part of the message was contained in one line: 'THE 1970 TOUR WAS ON'. There was an almost unprecedented chorus of cheers and counter-cheers when that was announced in the Long Room the following evening. By a strange lapse of security Peter Hain had been admitted to the press conference to hear it.

This meeting of the Council had been called following a debate over the whole issue in Parliament. Then, the government spokesmen, Jim Callaghan among them, had made it clear that the responsibility for decision lay with the Cricket Council. There would be no doubt, Mr Callaghan indicated, that the police could control any demonstrations; however, the Cricket Council had been urged to call off the tour. Representatives of the Council had been present to hear every word of the debate in which both sides of the problem had been skilfully presented. They had pondered long and they had decided now that the tour was still to go ahead.

The debate in the Commons had taken place in the last session of Parliament. There was to be a general election during the third week of June, and the South African tourists were to arrive on 1 June. It looked as though a real test of law and order under Labour was in the offing. Clearly, the government could not let it rest there.

The Home Secretary called for representatives of the Cricket Council to meet him on 19 May. Following the meeting, at which the Cricket Council were represented by Maurice Allom and Billy Griffith, the Council received a letter from the Home Secretary, the last paragraph of which contained a formal request from HM Government for the tour to be called off. On

22 May the Council announced that they felt they had no alternative but to accede to this request. With deep regret they had to announce that the tour was cancelled.

The outcome was to many of us a bitter disappointment for many reasons, not least because it led to the isolation of South Africa's cricketers as representatives of their country. Moreover, as we saw it, the rule of threatened mob violence had won the day. Yet, as near as dammit, it was the government who had been responsible for calling off the tour.

The evening before the Home Secretary sent for representatives of the Cricket Council for that final meeting, I was having an evening meal in a curry place close to Scotland Yard. My companions were three members of Special Branch, one of whom I had been in touch with for some time, another being, so he said, high up in the Peter Hain organization. They were feeling relieved: they had heard on the grapevine that the tour was to be called off – one way or another.

I think those of us close to the centre of things had all realized that to sustain a tour would be virtually impossible. But at least we had got so far as ensuring that the government had become closely involved in the cancellation.

In June that year the General Election was held. Polling took place on what had been scheduled as the first day of the Lord's Test and the Conservative party, speaking from a platform one of whose main planks was Law and Order, gained a narrow victory, much to the surprise of some of the pollsters.

Much has happened on the South African front since then. Without success, MCC members called upon the Committee to send a team to South Africa at a meeting which filled Central Hall, Westminster in 1982, and the ICC have annually debated the issue in one form or another ever since. In 1989, these discussions culminated in collective action against cricketers pursuing their profession in South Africa.

4

A TIME OF CHANGE

T HE CHANGES WHICH had taken place in 1968 with the formation of the Cricket Council and the Test and County
Cricket Board, had coincided with a resurgence in the game's
prosperity and popularity. This had had some connection with
the new structure at the top of the game's governance, but a
great deal more could be laid at the door of a more professional
approach to promoting, selling and publicizing cricket; the introduction of more one-day cricket; and a new-found willingness
on the part of the county clubs to consider the surgery necessary
for this to take place.

Between 1968 and 1974, the two-tier structure, with the Test
and County Cricket Board reporting to the Cricket Council
and with the Council taking responsibility for all strategic decisions on behalf of the game as a whole, had generally worked
pretty well. The responsible attitude and collective experience
of MCC, who were in the majority on the Council, had been
acknowledged. During this period, the Cricket Council had con-
sisted of representatives of the TCCB, the newly formed

National Cricket Association (NCA) and MCC. The TCCB, on which MCC had two votes but the county clubs one each (the Minor Counties had an aggregate of two), was now responsible to the Cricket Council for the first-class game and for the NCA, which had sprung directly from the old MCC Youth Cricket Association and like its forebear was responsible for the nourishment of the game at grass roots level.

These changes had taken place because Denis Howell, when Labour's Minister for Sport, had insisted that an amateur body, outside MCC and as part of a democratic body (the Cricket Council), could be the only possible recipient of grant aid from government sources. For a long time, the new 'democracy', to which MCC had in a sense sold its birthright, attracted precious little in the way of government funds. But the die had been cast and there was no going back.

In fact, during those six years, cricket was still controlled to a great extent by MCC. The Secretary of MCC was also Secretary of the Cricket Council and of the TCCB and to all intents and purposes of the NCA. MCC employed all the assistant secretaries working on behalf of MCC, TCCB, NCA and the Cricket Council. And the President of the Cricket Council was automatically the President of the NCA, and the Treasurer of MCC was ex officio Vice-chairman of that body.

However, by 1973 discussions had taken place within the Cricket Council, TCCB and MCC, and management consultants had been brought in to advise the Cricket Council on the structure and management of cricket at the highest level. As a consequence of these discussions MCC now held only a third of the voting power on the Cricket Council, though it retained two votes out of twenty-one on the Test and County Cricket Board. The most important and far-reaching changes, however, lay on the professional side of the new administrative arrangements for the first-class game. Donald Carr, properly ambitious and a dedicated administrator, was the first Secretary of the Cricket Council and of the TCCB who was not also employed by MCC. He had been an assistant secretary of MCC and he occupied offices at Lord's, the home of MCC, but now his prime loyalties lay elsewhere.

Whether looked at from the point of view of the Cricket Council, the TCCB or indeed the International Cricket Conference, MCC was an anomaly in an increasingly egalitarian framework. A private club with a public function it had always been, and for a very long time it had for all practical purposes held the reins, however lightly, which guided cricket along its path. Now it was the odd man out. As a member of the TCCB, it was the only club which did not run, or benefit financially from running, a county team. Middlesex were based at Lord's but were not structurally part of MCC. Teams still went abroad on major Test tours bearing the name and colours of MCC but MCC were no longer responsible for administering those tours, though through the President for a year, and through the Secretary, they were responsible for hosting, guiding and administering the International Cricket Conference.

The members of MCC owned Lord's cricket ground. A committee, elected by the membership, was charged under the rules of the Club with the sole right to administer the Club and all its functions, including all cricket matches played there. A large part of the time and energy of the Secretary, three assistant secretaries and a staff varying between sixty, all the year round, and eighty in the summer, was dedicated to that purpose.

In 1974, MCC, through Lord's, was the national and international headquarters of the game. The membership, then at 16,000, was international in composition and the life-blood of the Club's prosperity, both financially and in terms of prestige. The Club was by far the greatest source of income to cricket in the UK, not only because more games were played at Lord's than anywhere else but, more important, because in a five Test match season, one Test at Lord's produced up to 40 per cent of the total to be distributed from gate receipts. Ironically, the Club's own finances were in no sense healthy, for all the money from newly found sponsorship went to the counties.

MCC employees felt privileged to serve the Club, but they were not well paid.

Contemplating the future, as I then was, it seemed that MCC still had a vital individual role to play for the good of cricket at home and overseas. To do so meant holding on to the basic principles by which the Club had been administered throughout its history and which had stood the test of time. Only thus, did it seem to me, could MCC retain an influence for lasting good within the game and at the same time keep faith with its members.

As we have seen, the formation of the new administrative system had gone hand-in-hand with other radical changes, and the 1968–74 era had been one of the most revolutionary in the history of the game. The loosening of restrictions on overseas players in the county game, the introduction of large chunks of commercial sponsorship, allied to a drastic revision of the domestic programme to include more one-day cricket had all had their impact on the finances of county clubs and cricket at large.

Now, MCC's main functions administratively were to act responsibly through its role in international cricket, to maintain Lord's as the game's headquarters internationally, and to serve its members and public alike, by seeking excellence in performance from those responsible for running the place. Through its staff and under the direction of the MCC Committee, Lord's could and should remain the 'Premier Club'. Staging the best matches was part of it. Staging them from top to bottom better than anyone else was essential. Above all, the genuine cricketing public should be looked after.

Gimmicks, and short cuts, dubious methods and promotions in pursuit of the quick buck should be deflected if there was any danger of falling short of the highest standards. It would mean immense attention to detail from the time the first ticket was sold for any match to the time the last ball was bowled. It would mean a lot of hard work, but there would be reward in the fact of a job well done.

A Time of Change

Before applying for the post of Secretary of MCC, I had weighed the position carefully. MCC's authority at Lord's was not in doubt though the wider responsibilities of the TCCB had been properly established for some time. I knew, or thought I knew, the way they operated; knew the people involved; had spent seven years working for the game, in harness with them. Within my own orbit had been the marketing and public relations men, such as Raman Subba Row and Bernie Coleman of Surrey; Mike Turner of Leicestershire and Derrick Robbins of Warwickshire, Banbury Buildings Ltd, Coventry City football club and much else besides.

I had grown to recognize the talents of other administrators who would still be in key positions: Cecil Paris, Chairman of the Board since its inception, Edmund King of Warwickshire who chaired the committee responsible for distributing the TCCB's finances, and a whole host of other amateur administrators in the counties were colleagues and friends. In the same way, the county secretaries – in those days mostly former amateur first-class cricketers – generally approved of me and my work as far as I could see.

Sponsorship and other activities within my orbit had brought substantial income to county clubs that hitherto had languished. Just coming through now were the benefits of the way the mighty spending power of sponsoring companies had been harnessed into below-the-line advertising and promotion. All this was in addition to the instant rewards, financial and promotional, resulting from sometimes difficult negotiations.

Furthermore, these benefits to the game had been accomplished without prejudicing the integrity, the autonomy if you like, of the individual clubs which constituted the first-class game, or indeed of MCC. The first-class game was run by the TCCB; the individual clubs controlled their own destiny. The sole rights of the sponsors were invested in identification with the competition they supported. Individual grounds, including Lord's, did everything they could for the sponsors, in the way of entertainment and so forth; and, in general, did it very well.

But all this lay outside any contracted obligation and was much the better for that. The TCCB appeared to have reached the ideal position of a sort of EEC with no loss of sovereignty to individual members, but with a sensible approach to marketing those things held in common.

English cricket, for so long the Cinderella in the world of sport, was now showing a new vitality. Hand in hand with lucrative sponsorship deals and increased television coverage, came a gradual increase in the amount of press coverage. The quality papers had always given prominence to a game which more than any other seemed to lend itself to subtlety in reporting and commentary. Now there was something for popular tastes in the minds of editors of Fleet Street's popular press. Cricket had always been a game for and of the people, but had lost ground in the competition for space in the columns of the mass-circulation dailies. Led by the new *Sun*, with Frank Nicklin as sports editor, the proper reporting of cricket gradually made its way into the back pages of every newspaper, winter and summer.

For seven years I had been at the heart of change. As assistant secretary of MCC with important duties for the private club, I had spent more than 70 per cent of my time working in a commercial and public relations sense for the first-class game, and within that framework for the TCCB. I had grown to respect the capacity for hard work and the visionary qualities of Raman Subba Row. I also learned that beneath a warm and friendly exterior there lurked a certain ruthlessness. If a few elderly corns had been trodden on during the process of change, no important boundaries had been violated. I thought I knew just where the world of cricket stood and what MCC's place within that world should be. My days of service to the game at large, and to MCC and world cricket in particular, were taking different paths, but they were enchanced, so I thought, rather than limited.

This was a view that appeared to be shared by Messrs Allen, Mann and Davies when they interviewed me for the post of

Secretary of MCC. The job had been advertised, consultants had been employed and had made their recommendations. I left the MCC Committee Room, having read the advertisement for the job, having been assessed by the consultants, having been thoroughly quizzed and briefed by those at the interview and having established that the task of running Lord's at all times would be mine and that I would be responsible for this solely to the MCC Committee.

I have been asked, more times than I care to remember, to explain the workings of MCC and the job of the Secretary. I have found it impossible to do so to my own satisfaction. By the time you have touched on all the ramifications the listener's eyes have, likely as not, tended to glaze over.

As far as I was concerned, during nearly thirteen years spent in attempting to do it, the job was potentially the best job in the world. You had to feel that, otherwise there was no point in starting. On the other hand, because of its theoretical (but not practical) potential, it was full of frustrations. You knew what you wanted to achieve for the Club, for cricket; you sought and got agreement for your plans from the Committee but likely as not it would always take a titanic effort to make a small amount of progress. This was inevitable with the Committee system applied to a multi-faceted club like MCC.

The profit motive has a certain simplicity which reasonable management can achieve and be judged by. This works in business. But in an organization like MCC so many other factors, including the almost indefinable 'the good of cricket' about which varying valid ideas are held, are bound to be considered. These are more or less important to different individuals.

Yet for all sorts of reasons rule by Committee is the only answer for dealing with an intelligent, sometimes critical membership and with the wider responsibilities that come from owning Lord's cricket ground. Furthermore, MCC has been fortunate in being able to call upon a wide range of expertise from top men in their field with knowledge not only of their subject but, just as important, where to go, to whom to go for help and advice.

The relationship of the MCC Committee with the Secretariat and staff of the club could best be described as one of benevolent, extremely benevolent, despotism. It would be misleading to compare it with the old role of amateurs and professionals in the cricketing sense, although the comparison is not wholly inappropriate. At different times, on different days, with different people on the Committee, I could run through a whole gamut of parts; friend, adviser, advised, instructor, instructed, servant, respected Secretary. It was the nature of the job and a symptom of its elasticity. With very few exceptions, however, was business conducted with less than time-honoured respect on both sides or in the most civilized manner.

In my time the Secretary of MCC was designated in the rules of the Club as an officer, together with the President (for the time being), the Treasurer and the Chairman of Finance. The responsibility for the management of the affairs of the Club was invested in the Committee. The Committee were responsible to the members for the conduct of the affairs of the Club. Lord's was and is owned by the members – 18,000 of them, give or take a few.

The Secretary was the head of the executive arm and as such was responsible for the delegation of responsibility to the assistant secretaries and all other members of the sixty-strong staff. He was also responsible for all correspondence on behalf of the Club, whether from his own office or from the office of another member of staff, to whom he had to delegate various duties.

The Committee's chief responsibility was to lay down policy, and the Secretary was bound to act within the areas of that policy. It was also his function to advise the Committee on alternative policies available to them in various instances. In order to do this he had to be an authority on all details concerning the role of the Club past and present, and he needed to have an eye to the future. He had to be aware of the precedents by which the Club operated and from time to time remind the

Committee, so that they were aware of those precedents and principles by which the Club had survived and flourished. As the only officer of the Club who was paid and was working for perhaps ten hours a day, sometimes seven days a week, he was expected by most Committee members to be an authority on the workings of the Club and of the functions of others who likewise spent long hours in the service of MCC and of Lord's. It was usually to him and to his colleagues on the Secretariat that members came for advice, for help or to complain. As with the membership, so with the staff, all of whom were dedicated to MCC and to the game of cricket.

The duties of each member of staff must still involve coping with the inebriated and bellicose as well as the decent and polite. More often than not their duties involve long, anti-social hours and a great many more kicks than ha'pence. They are most fully rewarded when the sun shines, the ground is full, a great game of cricket is being played and the crowd is genuinely and utterly absorbed by what goes on in the middle of the most famous cricket ground in the world. It is moments like these that atone for the days when the weather goes wrong, when the public are out of sorts and blaming all on the staff. Theirs is a job connected with the most unpredictable and vulnerable game ever invented and most of the time it is carried out under the critical gaze of the cricketing public. But if the rewards are rare, they are the greater for that. During my time as Secretary of MCC, Lord's was extremely fortunate with its staff and, I'm glad to say, by the time I left most of them were being paid somewhere near what they were worth.

The administration of Lord's with its large membership, as a centre for the playing of cricket, real tennis and squash, with its responsibilities as a nursery for young cricketers, a fixture-list for members of nearly 250 games a season, the staging of one or two Test matches a year and two Cup finals; and with the added responsibilities of being 'live-in' landlords to Middlesex and the TCCB, has always been a hectic affair. This is largely because a considerable number of people are rightly and reasonably involved in the policy-making which dictates how the place is run, and not all their ideas are by any means similar.

MCC depends greatly on its committee structure. At the top is a Committee consisting of fifteen members elected by the members of the Club, plus the chairmen of five of the eight or so sub-committees which consider specific areas of Club's affairs, together with the officers of the Club. The sub-committees meet regularly to agendas prepared by the Secretariat. The Treasurer is a key figure in the whole operation, being the senior long-serving non-executive. The President takes the chair at meetings, but is in office for only one year and in the normal course of events would greatly heed the advice of the Treasurer, the Chairman of Finance, and the Secretary. The Secretary may from time to time consult the Treasurer and other officers if seeking help or advice on particular matters which are outside policy already laid down but which require immediate action.

The buck stops with the MCC Committee, or at least it used to, for everything which happened at Lord's. They had the power, through themselves or their appointed representatives (usually the Treasurer and Secretary), to decide and dispense, to advise and consent on any matter connected with Lord's cricket ground, and they were entrusted by the membership of the Club with just those responsibilities.

Yet the one continuing thread is the Secretary of MCC. I always felt keenly my responsibility to the MCC Committee as their executive arm and to the International Cricket Conference in the same way.

But there was more, much more to it than that. It was important that one's colleagues and staff saw in the Secretary someone who would champion any just cause of theirs before Committee, others in the cricket world and members of the public. This did not simply mean ensuring that those who worked for MCC were reasonably paid. There was the question of protecting the dignity of the individual, so that his job satisfaction, however meagre, was given as much scope as possible.

Fairness, it always seemed to me, was vital. Popularity was

desirable but took second place to integrity and the ability to fight for the right cause, based on the great traditions of Lord's and a need to move with the times without being trendy.

Often this would mean persuading individuals, on the Committee or elsewhere, that their own special views were, while brilliant in themselves, not necessarily compatible with the overall aims and objectives already laid down and in train.

During my own time at Lord's my sanity was often saved by the wisdom shown by the MCC Committee in allowing the staff and me to get on with the executive process without hands-on interference. There were exceptions to the rule, but these were few and far between. This meant that we could plan and execute, and stand or fall on performance, when it came to the big occasion. It was this understanding attitude to our needs and aspirations that kept us going in times of trouble. And, given all the circumstances, the results were good.

One aspect of life on those major match days, when the ground was full and the big occasion was upon us and the TV and radio pundits were in full flow, was the bomb warning. I mention this only because it serves to illustrate the need for a chain of command on such occasions which brooks no interference. As the Secretary I was responsible for deciding whether or not to evacuate the ground when a bomb-warning was telephoned or otherwise received at Lord's.

This happened probably ten times during my term of office. After the first bomb-warning my predecessor had understandably evacuated the ground. It was a new phenomenon, then, and he felt bound to act – as anyone would have done in the circumstances.

Following that historic day in 1973, a strict routine was drawn up with the aid of the police. It was adhered to strictly and everyone on the ground knew what to do in given circumstances. Fortunately, on each of these ten or so occasions, the warning got no further than me and the Commander or Chief Superintendent in charge of police on the day. Careful cognizance was taken of the nature and method of the warning, the location of the so-called bomb. Each time the vulnerability of the ground had to be taken into account, alongside the nature of the information received. Each time, with the final decision in my hands, but acting after deep consultation with the police, it was decided to take no action. Each time, thank God, we were right. The contest went on with nobody else the least bit disturbed. Quite rightly the MCC Committee never questioned the authority of the Secretary in making such day-to-day decisions. Left to ourselves we made a good team.

When dealing with MCC's vast club membership I often found it useful to imagine the type of man I would most like to please – my ideal member in other words. He would be old-fashioned in many ways, steeped in cricked lore; as honest as the day is long; prejudiced, perhaps, but certainly not intolerant; not wealthy but staunchly middle-class in the old-fashioned sense.

It may have been just one such member who, during the 1973 bomb scare, was found making his way towards the car-park, against all instructions (for all anyone knew it was there that the bomb was to be found). Prevented from going to his car by an MCC steward, he objected strongly. The steward pointed out the dangers. 'Precisely,' agreed the member. 'That's why I must get to my car. I am 70 years of age and my car's worth a damned sight more than I am.'

5

ON THE ROAD TO KERRY

As my time as assistant, later deputy, secretary drew to an end and I prepared to take up my new appointment as Secretary of MCC in June 1974, there was sense of some achievement, but with new worlds still to conquer, old worlds to maintain, despite the knowledge that in the Cricket Council MCC's influence had begun to wane and that elements within TCCB sought far-reaching changes. During the next twelve years those changes would all but extinguish MCC's authority even at Lord's.

When I took up office I soon realised that little would be straightforward or capable of clear definition for some time to come. The role of the MCC Committee and of the Secretary in respect of Lord's cricket ground was even then being questioned by some important figures in the game, just as the role of the Club itself in the wider world of cricket had to be shaped and, if necessary, defended.

One area of responsibility with which I had been entrusted in my new role was that of Secretary of the International Cricket

Conference. The ICC had been in the past almost wholly a forum for discussion. Meetings had been held annually in July to discuss matters of common interest and individuals representing member countries had listened and spoken and then on the whole gone back home to do their own thing. Yes, there were rules of the Conference and rules relating to some aspects of the playing of cricket at international level. And yes, individual countries subscribed to them. The creation of any real and unifying impetus within the framework of ICC was, understandably, extremely difficult. Australia, for instance, did not want Pakistan, West Indies or anyone else interfering in, or creating mandates which they thought might interfere with, the best interests of Australian cricket. There was, and always will be, a natural reluctance on the part of those intimately concerned with their own territory and the prosperity of cricket within it, to yield authority for any but the most general issues to an international body. It is the same the whole world over, in any walk of life.

The first-ever World Cup was staged in 1975. It was hugely successful and it was played throughout in the most generous spirit. It was played under the auspices of the ICC, organized extremely well on their behalf by the English authorities and, at that stage, with Prince Philip as Chairman of ICC and President of MCC, any question of who was responsible for what happened at Lord's was not at issue.

The final of the Cup was held at Lord's, and the cricket played by West Indies and Australia graced the occasion. The momentum provided by the impact of the one-day game on English cricket had without doubt reached the world arena. There was then no international embracing of the one-day game, as there is now; and the World Cup as a whole, and that final in particular, was a catalyst from which many future triumphs and troubles were to spring.

Even during the three weeks which encompassed the competition in 1975, I had encountered an attitude which I did not then understand, but which in retrospect could, and perhaps should, have been seen as significant for the future.

The arrival of the World Cup teams had been marked by a photograph session at Lord's, followed by a huge buffet luncheon. Everyone was there. Each team had been allocated its own table. The captains of all the teams and one or two others had been given a place at a table at which sat the President of MCC, Prince Philip. Everything had gone smoothly. I suppose I was in a self-congratulatory frame of mind. Then I noticed that two places on the President's table were vacant. As I cast round the assembled throng, the captains of Australia and West Indies put in a late appearance.

'Thank heaven,' I said, 'please grab some food. You are sitting over there.' I indicated the two vacant seats.

It quickly became plain that neither individual was remotely interested in sitting where I had indicated. They did not, they said, have any interest in 'that sort of thing'. I pointed out that, as guests, they should either take the seats they had been allocated, or offend their hosts, but it was several seconds before they agreed to take up their appointed places. It had been a nasty moment, and it shook me.

The game had changed. Sponsorship and television – particularly television – had created a new stature for the international cricketer. In his own mind, the professional was now a star to rank alongside the other well-known personalities appearing on the magic box. Yet in their eyes, the authorities had not recognized this sufficiently well to merit their respect. The top players were now being represented by agents, and these agents, not unnaturally, extolled the worth of their clients and put them in the way of off-the-field activities more lucrative than ever before. The star syndrome was upon us, and in some cases it was being represented by boorish behaviour. Why else were Australian players openly complaining about the restrictions placed on their off-the-field activities by the Australian Board, which, I believed, thoroughly understood the players' pretensions and were doing their best in going as far as they could to meet them. Indeed Bob Parish, Chairman of the Australian Board, told us they were concerned about the need to bridge the widening gap between administrators and players and were forming a special sub-committee which would contain the captains of the various States. This committee was set up early in the 1976–77 Australian season.

In England, relations between administrators and the Cricketers' Association were good. The Association took a responsible view of all cricket in the country. They went a long way down the road of recognizing a duty to all cricket from the grass roots upwards. They made sure that their players had a reasonable share of the cake, but they also saw that the cricket they wanted to play was capable of producing only one cake, one which had to be cut into a large number of portions. This did not, however, mean that individual English cricketers at the highest levels aspired to less than their Australian counterparts, or that money, or what some saw as lack of it, was not often at the forefront of their minds.

Throughout the world, cricketers were generally loyal to the Establishment in their country, and not just because there was nowhere else to go. Mostly it was recognized that administrators did their best for the game with little reward, even if, sometimes, that best was, in the players' eyes, a poor one. Different countries had their own problems. West Indies cricket had precious little money to distribute. India attracted vast gates but were beset by currency restrictions which affected the itinerant cricketer. Pakistan cricket was heavily sponsored but government connections were strong in a poor country. In New Zealand, the cult of the professional had not bitten deep and their comparative isolation had built a sense of strong patriotic pride among their cricketing fraternity.

At home, Tony Greig had become England's captain. A man of charisma, he was larger than life in every way. Tall and blond, a gifted if not superlative all-rounder, he overcame his deficiencies with an attacking yet responsible approach to everything connected with the game – on or off the field. To those watching England play in those days, Greig personified a fresh and much needed élan which, after an unsuccessful period, produced an almost tangible fighting spirit. A 'gorgeous man' to the peripherally interested female, he brought a touch of the Second World War fighter ace back to the British public. And he played it to the hilt.

His first real success as captain came in India in 1976–77 when he led the team which won a series for the first time since Douglas Jardine had done so in 1933–34. To the Indian crowds he was more than a man. This tall Greek god of a figure, with a superb sense of public relations and, now, a winning way on the field, almost made those millions from Bombay to Calcutta forget that their team was being beaten. His was a triumphal tour in every way.

The MCC Committee kindly agreed that the President, Tagge Webster, an absolutely straight, blunt gentleman of the old-fashioned school, and I should accept an invitation from the Australians to attend the Centenary Test match between Australia and England which followed the India tour. And it was agreed that we should also visit some of the other Test match playing countries, as Chairman and Secretary of ICC.

We flew out in February 1977, headed for Bombay. India, Pakistan, Singapore and then Australia were on the first part of our itinerary, and wherever we went we were treated much like royalty. It was a tiring, happy, wonderful experience; and we learned a lot.

We did not catch up with Tony Greig and his team until we arrived in Perth, Western Australia. They were there for a three-day match prior to the Centenary Test in Melbourne and we met first at a reception given by the Governor of Western Australia. The England team were impressive. They were all dressed in their MCC blazers (those, incidentally, were the days when the MCC label went with the touring team) and as Tagge Webster said later to me, they looked like a team. In contrast to much that had taken place in previous years, when a reaction against being 'properly dressed' had been paramount, here was a spirit of quiet pride, doubtless instilled by the captain, and we were wholly won over by the greeting given to us by him and his team. Dear old Tagge was delighted, and full of praise for the Greig outlook.

Nor was this impression much dented by tales of mercenary dealings in India, quite out of keeping with past tours out there, which we now heard from newspapermen who had accompanied the side. The poverty of many followers of cricket from the public stands at every Indian venue is all too well known. In the past, requests for autographs, miniature cricket bats and the like had been met freely. The journalists expressed their disappointment at the way in which the MCC players had seemed to squeeze every last penny out of their popularity, even down to selling autographed cricket bats to children at the grounds and charging for photographs being taken at various functions.

Somehow, though, the euphoria embracing that first 'all's right with the world' feeling that captured our imagination when we arrived in Australia overcame all else. It was a time for celebrating a hundred years of cricket between Australia and England and for meeting a posse of old friends. Our warm reception when we arrived in Melbourne, and the sheer delight of sharing it all with so many cricketing friends, the match itself and everything that went with it, the whole camaraderie of the cricket world . . . nothing could shake that, and nothing did. Not then.

What nobody knew – no Australian administrator, no English administrator, no administrator in the wide world – was that even as we basked in the warmth of our own contentment, a deal had already been struck by some of those playing in that Centenary Test. It was a deal similar to that which would shortly be sealed in complete secrecy by other players. It was to shake international cricket to its foundations. It became known later as the Packer affair.

My tour with the President continued as, accompanied by Gubby Allen, we did a whistle-stop tour of New Zealand from

North Island to South. The New Zealand Cricket Council had put themselves out enormously for our visit. Walter Hadlee, Gordon Burgess, John Heslop, Bob Knowles were all marvellously hospitable, and when we arrived back in England there was a visit from the Australians to look forward to. Domestic politics receded into the distant past. We were looking forward with fond hopes and keen expectation to the summer to come. After all, England appeared to have found the right captain and the Australians were vulnerable. The previous summer had seen England thrashed by the West Indies, but enough of all that. There was a buzz of expectancy in the air at Lord's. Before long there was an expectancy of a different kind. It was hushed and it was bewildered.

My own first knowledge that a predator had invaded our nice, enclosed garden in which everything seemed to be coming on well was when I read the newspapers on the morning of 9 May 1977. Tony Greig had given a press conference at Hove and had announced that: 'A massive cricket project is under way involving most of the world's top players'. He had admitted that he was part of it, along with a number of England players. A full announcement was to be made later that week.

The fullest account was in the *Daily Mail*, which appeared to have knowledge to which others were not privy. It was easy to see why, in retrospect, but at that time nobody knew that Richie Benaud, former Australian captain and distinguished commentator on the game, a close friend of Ian Woolridge of the *Mail*, was a guiding light in the entourage of Kerry Packer. 'Kerry who?' I asked myself at the time. In due course I was to find out.

At this precise time, I knew nothing of any problems the Australian Cricket Board may have had with the granting of television rights in Australia, and no more than I have already outlined about the dissatisfaction with their rewards among the top players in the world. In England it was the province of the TCCB; overseas, other authorities kept their financial affairs under wraps. That they should do so was even written into the ICC Rules.

For all I knew then, this 'massive' project Greig had spoken of, with its implied threat, could have been a matter capable of a domestic resolution. But there seemed to be no harm in preparing the ground. I contacted the Chairman of ICC and obtained his consent to writing to Test match playing countries – all of them – to discuss the matter under the auspices of the International Cricket Conference. Even then it seemed imperative that there should be a united course of action within the world of Test cricket, if the need arose, and if matters took an ugly turn. It could well be that the Conference would have its uses after all.

Packer's own magazine – the *Bulletin* – published more details later in the same week that the first inklings had become known. It talked of a 54-day programme to take place in Australia in their summer of 1977. Mention was made that thirty-five of the world's best cricketers would be taking part. Contracts had been signed for one to three years (so it was not only the following summer that would be affected). The package had been arranged between J. P. Sport and the proprietors of Channel 9. It seemed the whole of the Packer empire and its considerable resources would be involved.

The UK Cricket Council acted quickly on the one subject with which they were certain of their ground. Greig had in their eyes betrayed English cricket. The captain of England had dealt the game that nourished him a stab in the back. He was, after all, a member of the cricket establishment in the UK, so the thinking went. Not only had his actions 'not been cricket', but they had been treacherous. It has to be recognized that, rightly or wrongly, cricket was seen by those who administered it as *their* province; theirs by tradition, by virtue of the time that they gave to it, by the unspoken agreement of millions, by the experience they, mainly as former players, brought to the game. Greig's action in signing for Packer and, worse still, using the inside track given to him by his captaincy of England to act as agent in signing other players, was deplored. Morality and loyalty were large issues in what they saw as the ethos of the game. They had nursed a viper in their bosom.

These were the sort of unspoken feelings running through the minds of those who sat round the Committee Room table at Lord's. I was not at the meeting of the Cricket Council which discussed the matter of the England captaincy, for both the Chairman of ICC and I felt, I think rightly, that as officers of world rather than English cricket we should remain outside the domestic fray for the time being. The words the Council chose to convey their decision wisely understated their real feelings.

> 'The captaincy of the England team involves close liaison with the selectors in the management, selection and development of England players for the future, and clearly Tony Greig is unlikely to undertake this as his stated intention is to be contracted elsewhere during the next three winters. . . . His action has clearly impaired the trust which existed between the authorities and the captain of the England side.'

This statement was made and acted upon before the full facts of Packer's ultimate intentions were known, either to the cricket authorities or probably to Packer himself. It was difficult to avoid the temptation of thinking that Packer would go away. How could he sustain and organize worthwhile cricket matches in Australia? It was as if he did not understand that 'authorised cricket' held the world copyright on the game and its organization. It was soon to become obvious that Packer would be a dangerous man to under-rate; but under-rate him and misread his intentions we did.

By the time the Cricket Council had pronounced on Greig and the England captaincy, all Test match countries had been written to. I had outlined the position as it was thought to be and had asked whether they felt it would be a good idea to meet, both as a body to discuss the latest turn of events, and, if it proved possible, with Kerry Packer and/or his representatives so that ICC would know precisely what it was up against. Rumour and speculation were rife. Before action of any irrevocable kind was taken, it was essential that as much hard information as possible was to hand. Even at this stage, voices in English cricket were opposed to bringing the ICC into the affair. 'It's a domestic Australian issue into which English cricket has been dragged,' I was told. Nevertheless I wrote, and nevertheless the member countries sensibly agreed that such a meeting should be held.

The Cricket Council had met on 13 May 1977, and as a result Greig had been deposed. On 26 May it was announced that all cricketers, whether reported to have signed for Packer or not, would be available for selection in the coming series against Australia. It was of course well known by then that the Australian team contained a number of players who were contracted by Packer.

An emergency meeting of ICC representatives was held on 14 June and it was agreed that I should take steps to invite Packer to a meeting at the earliest possible date. Representatives were also acquainted with all that was known of the position at that time, including a difference of opinion between Packer and the Australian Board about the television rights for Test cricket in Australia. Just how important a factor this was, did not become apparent at that time.

The catalogue of many of the events of that summer of 1977 are well known to most cricket followers. The series for the Ashes was a one-sided contest. Australia were a divided team with a management in the form of Len Maddocks and Norman McMahon who had no sympathy for the aspirations of those who had signed for Packer. The overwhelming weight of the cricketing public was against those in the Packer camp. It was in this atmosphere − seething with speculation as to whether the Packer players might see the folly of their ways; whether Packer was pulling an enormous bluff in order to get TV rights for cricket; and much trotting to and fro between Lord's and various legal chambers − that the meeting with Packer was held.

At the time all we knew was that a series was planned between Australia and the Rest of the World (led by Tony Greig) and that sufficient players had been signed up for that purpose. They had been signed in absolute secrecy, but they had been signed. There was no doubt about that.

Packer had already appeared in England. His whole attitude had been that of someone who was simply helping the world's top cricketers to get their just desserts. The cricket authorities, especially those in Australia, were described as people who simply did not understand the modern world. He had expressed a willingness to talk with them, however, and this had given us a cue. Packer had also appeared on David Frost's programme in a live debate against opposition which could have been hand-picked by Packer, not for the allegiances of those chosen, certainly not, but because none of them got to the real heart of the matter. David Frost, who had strong business ties with Packer's Channel 9, was hardly, on the evidence of that programme, a chairman whose impartiality could be guaranteed. But it was a well staged show and it put Packer and his aspirations in a sympathetic light.

Our timing in arranging a meeting with Packer was not greatly helped by the fact that on the very day that ICC agreed that one should be organized, he decided to embark for New York. It seemed a deliberate move to put us in the wrong for not having contacted him before, but I had had no brief to do so before our meeting. As soon as the meeting finished I contacted the London office of Consolidated Press, a central part of the Packer empire, only to learn of his disappearance. In due course through that office and by means of their contact with him in New York, a meeting was arranged for 23 June.

It is worth recording the state of affairs in the camp of 'authorized cricket' at the time of the meeting with Kerry Packer. In cricketing terms he was an unprecedented threat. How great a threat we could not know. We had spent years nurturing the game from top to bottom, had found a broad basis of agreement about how it should be administered (though we had problems in always agreeing). At every level it was on an upward curve through the joint efforts of players and administrators. Traditional aspects of the game had been always to the forefront. Preserving the best of the old, even in the mini-revolution of one-day cricket that had taken place, had seemed of vital importance. Not only did Packer appear to be threatening these traditions, but he was a threat (let's be honest) to the self-esteem of those representing established cricket, and not simply because he had fallen out with our friends and allies the Australian Cricket Board.

Because I had not been involved in preliminary discussions between those representing English and Australian cricket, the precise extent of the row in Australia which had led to our present problems was unclear. The same could be said for the Chairman. As far as was possible, after acres of newsprint and untold media speculation, we were in a position to approach the meeting with Packer with an open mind as to which outcome would be best for cricket. A provisional programme of matches had been devised, which it was hoped would go some way to giving Packer a series of matches which could be televised by Channel 9, be accorded first-class status, and at the same time give the Australian Board a chance to fulfil their obligations to the Australian Broadcasting Commission during a series with India, even though they were thoroughly compromised by the suggested schedule. It was a formula for co-existence.

The Packer party, apart from himself, comprised David McNicholl of Consolidated Press, whose services I had used in keeping track of Packer to arrange the meeting, Lynton Taylor formerly of BBC, now of Channel 9, and Richie Benaud. Richie Benaud! It was a shock to see him. There was no real reason to imagine that the former Australian captain, a friend to all of us sitting round that table and something of a hero to me, was different from anyone else, but did he really think he was on the right track? It was no consolation that he looked distinctly uncomfortable.

It was a strange meeting. Our initiative with the suggested

programme for the next Australian summer was discussed, but Packer (who did nearly all the talking on their side of the table) treated it in the most perfunctory way. He suggested that we could set up a joint working party to look at the programme. It then became clear that we had not yet reached the real point. Certainly not as far as Kerry Packer was concerned. It soon became apparent what the score was.

In addition to insisting that players who had signed to take part in his cricket should not be victimized, he came out with: 'I shall need a guarantee that Channel 9 will receive the exclusive television rights for Australian cricket after the 1978–79 season. That, gentlemen, is not negotiable.'

He suggested that perhaps we might like to discuss his proposal in private. It was agreed that he would look briefly around Lord's, and Packer and his party left the Committee Room. I saw them out and enquired if they would like anyone to show them round. They settled for Richie Benaud, who knew his way round Lord's as well as anybody.

Back in the Committee Room, the main discussion centered round Packer's last words. Had he *really* said that? We agreed that he had. The proposition was examined. It was really an Australian problem, but a problem which on the face of it seemed insoluble. How could they give such a guarantee in practical terms even if they had wanted to? And even if they could give a guarantee, would it be in the best interests of Australian cricket? Only they could judge. (No sum had been mentioned.) More important in the view of some of us was the whole question of whether allowing a television company to dictate the course of events could possibly be a basis for the present and future running of any aspect of cricket, let alone international cricket. Bob Parish, Chairman of the Australian Board and Ray Steele, the Treasurer, were clearly not of the opinion that such a possibility could be entertained. They had the full backing of those present, most of whom had been horrified by Packer's approach. The Australians, who had hitherto been firmly against exclusivity of television coverage for any Australian channel, said that they would certainly recommend to their Board that the question be considered seriously when the terms of the next contract was examined, and that Channel 9 should be given every opportunity to bid.

As I reclaimed Packer and his entourage from the Long Room, I was filled with dread as to what might be in store during the weeks, months, years ahead. But surely Packer realized how impossible his demands had been? Surely, he would not have come to Lord's merely to go through a charade, some sort of public relations exercise? There must be an answer somewhere. Perhaps there was a nuance that we had missed, a way out. If only we could find the key.

In Packer's view, it soon transpired, the key was to find a form of words. There was no shifting his position. Exclusive rights, or else. He was not going to stand in a queue with everyone else. Tagge Webster, the Chairman, after looking round the room at the grim faces assembled there, in a silent question as to whether anyone present wished to say more, thanked the Packer party for their time, and with typical politeness indicated that the meeting was at an end, unfortunately without agreement.

At a brief conference with the press waiting outside the pavilion, Packer revealed two things which indicated that the meeting had almost certainly been a public relations exercise after all. One was that he had signed an entire West Indies squad. This meant that nearly fifty players had been put under contract to him, not the thirty-five we had known about, and our proposals had been made in ignorance of this. The other was his philosophy. 'Let the devil take the hindmost,' he said, on his way through the Grace Gates.

The annual meeting of the International Cricket Conference was due to be held on 26 July. Before that date every possible step had to be taken, in the face of many unknown factors, to preserve traditional international cricket. It has been written that the member countries of ICC acted from a desire to punish the players who had 'betrayed the established game', but there was, to my mind, little of that sort of feeling in the air. Attitudes varied, of course, but paramount in the minds of those I knew well and conferred with in the next few difficult weeks, was at least one major objective: to defeat World Series Cricket so as best to preserve the game we knew for the game at large, not just for the benefit of today's and, in some cases, yesterday's heroes.

It seemed that reaching any sort of reasonable accommodation was impossible. The question now was how best to act with the maximum effect to prevent member countries of ICC from being picked off at will by an organization that had declared war primarily against Australia but had also, through ICC, declared war against us all. The only option to appear realistic at that time was 'to take arms against a sea of troubles, and by opposing, end them'.

Careful analysis, taking in the whole wide world of cricket, was difficult in those hectic days when it seemed that nearly every dawn produced another bombshell. Nor did we have the benefit of hindsight. True, various voices were raised urging a peaceful solution at any price, but they were few.

In England, the TCCB took up the running on behalf of UK cricket; the Australians, too, were well up to their eyes in legal opinions about their own domestic position. The TCCB met and were militant, perhaps beyond the realms of the legal advice that was offered them. Doug Insole was Chairman of the TCCB in those days, was the UK representative at the meeting of the ICC and was in complete sympathy with Australia, the other founder member.

I had received a statement, carefully drafted by counsel before that ICC meeting, held on 26 July, and the bulk of that day was spent in rehearsing the history of the problem, attempting to look into the future and forming a plan of action. That carefully worded statement finally won the approval of all member countries. It was direct and to the point.

Taking the press conference at Lord's that evening was an occasion when the adrenalin flowed fast. The cricket press of the world were present. There was no doubt that the English press would welcome the news I had to give, as would the Australians. In fact most of them would have felt downright disappointed if nothing positive had emerged, and we would have been castigated. What we had to say was certainly positive. Apart from re-affirming the view that the whole structure of world cricket could be severely damaged by the type of promotion proposed by Mr Packer and those associated with his venture, I went on to make the following points on behalf of the Conference: ICC were determined to continue to promote international cricket; Packer's matches would not be accorded first-class status, nor appear in official records; ICC had unanimously passed a change in their rules. These rules, I pointed out, came under the heading of Qualification for Test Matches. To the current rules should be added:

> 'No player who after October 1st 1977 has played or made himself available to play in a match previously disapproved by the Conference shall thereafter be eligible to play in any Test match under the auspices of ICC.'

I then went on to spell out the type of promotions and persons of which the Conference disapproved. It was also made clear that all member countries of the Conference were urged to apply similar sanctions at first-class and domestic levels.

While I had been able to say that the decision had been unanimous, in so far as Test cricket was concerned, this unanimity had been hard won where the West Indies had been concerned. They had, in all fairness, put forward their misgivings at the meeting, fearing the effect if the decision was challenged, and also fearing, not unreasonably, the reactions of the people at home. For the ordinary man in the West Indies, Test match cricketers had the same aura about them as film stars. Signing with Packer was to them in much the same mould as changing studios for more money. The ties of friendship and support for the game to which they had given so much prevailed over the misgivings voiced by Jeffrey Stollmeyer and Allan Rae, however, and they supported the motion in the end. The fervour of the other delegates proved impossible to resist. They had voted and the vote had been unanimous, and, although criticized for it later, I would still maintain that it was my job only to convey the decision to the media, not the debate which had led to it. Nor, in my view, should we have given Packer the chance of exploiting any hint of an ICC which was anything other than united and resolute.

It was a tough time to have to live through. In a sense, the thorough grounding I had obtained by involvement with the d'Oliveira affair and the 1970 South African problems, and my familiarity with media matters, were all helpful. But as a comparatively new Secretary of MCC and of ICC I certainly felt that I was being put on my mettle. The constant hammering at MCC's door by the TCCB abated for a while out of sheer necessity, as we combined to serve the wider interests of the game. To that extent there was a merciful release on the one hand and a whole new weight of responsibility on the other. There was time for little else. When not answering enquiries from the press of the world – from Canada to Australia and most points between – I was occupied with the affairs of MCC and Lord's during a busy summer when it appeared that 'business as usual' was imposing a great strain on everybody at Lord's. As is the way with these things, the MCC Committee and the staff, though only involved peripherally in the wider issues, were wonderfully helpful and understanding.

It was during the monthly meeting of the MCC Committee, held on 2 August, that I received a telephone call from Packer's solicitors. Ironically, it came three days after I had led MCC in a celebratory match against Hambledon CC at Hambledon, the cradle of the game in England. I went with Oliver Popplewell QC to my office to learn of Packer's intention to seek an injunction against ICC and TCCB to prevent implementation of the new ICC rule and recommendations. Oliver was a great help then, and two days later when a hearing was held before Mr Justice Slynn, he was there, at the drop of a wig, to represent ICC interests.

CONFLICTS IN CRICKET

A vacation court, with barristers from other cases – a long stream of them – making representations to the judge, while we waited for our case to be heard, was far removed from my own recollections of my only previous experience, in the case with London Weekend Television. Now the air was filled with phrases like, 'My client and I have been waiting with our pads on for quite some time, M'Lud'. Or, 'I'm afraid our opponents have slipped in a bouncer, M'Lud, and it is unlikely that we shall be able to settle as anticipated'. The upshot of the two-day hearing was that Packer was unfortunately alerted to the draconian nature of the contracts he held with his players, and he immediately sent them covering letters correcting the matter. It was also agreed that no action would be taken by the cricket authorities to embark on their proposed course of action until a full hearing had taken place.

In effect no action would have been taken during the 1977 season in England anyway, but a few days later the TCCB announced their intention to ban from county cricket for two years those players who appeared for Packer in the forthcoming Australian season. It was in everyone's interest that a full hearing should be held as soon as possible. It was not long before we knew it was scheduled for 26 September, in the Chancery Division of the High Court. Sometime later, we learned that the judge would be Mr Justice Slade, brother of Julian, composer of *Salad Days*; the link with cricket lunches was all too tenuous to take as any kind of omen.

The trouble with writing about such happenings, to which everyone already knows the answer, is the immense difficulty of conveying what it was like when we didn't think we had done anything wrong.

Here we were, protecting cricket: part of the English heritage, now the world's heritage. A game in which honour was a byword, which had lent its name to phrases in common usage throughout the English-speaking world. We were bound to administer cricket from the lowest to the highest, and, in a manner of speaking, had been elected so to do. Recognized cricket had been sold down the river by a number of players. This had been arranged in great secrecy by the head of an Australian TV channel to enable him, in the first place, to have such a grip on the Australian Cricket Board that they would, against their better judgement, ensure him a lucrative business deal at the expense of his rivals by giving him exclusive rights to cover Australian cricket promoted by them. Surely, our case was a good one. We had acted to protect the game we were elected to administer. And we had all been in agreement on the action to be taken. I suppose that if I had been asked what I felt at that time I would have said that cricket was one of the constant bastions of the ideals we hoped the world would one day live by; that it was too precious not to preserve as we had tried to preserve it; that surely everyone could see that? The honour of representing your country could not be surpassed by all the money in the world.

By the time the case was heard, Doug Insole, Chairman of the TCCB, had announced the sponsorship of Test matches by Cornhill. It was an interesting piece of timing and as far as I am aware it was, in those whirling, fragmented days, negotiated without the full knowledge of the TCCB on whose behalf it was done. It certainly brought more money into established cricket, but had the effect in the minds of many of giving all the credit to Packer and his intrusion. That the sponsorship of Test cricket should have come about at this time, and with such obvious haste, and without proper consultation, and in spite of previous decisions that Test cricket was too prestigious to be sponsored, was at the very least a double-edged sword.

The two platforms on which the plaintiffs rested their case were inducement to breach of contract and unlawful restraint of trade.

It was quickly apparent that Packer had taken the greatest care in choosing his defendants among the cricketers. It was also apparent that when he signed certain of them it could have been done with just such a court case in mind. Named as plaintiffs were Tony Greig, John Snow and Mike Proctor. Snow was at the end of his career, and the inference was obvious: this was an opportunity for him to pick up some real money at last. Proctor was a marvellous cricketer, but as a South African he could not play Test cricket and here was Packer providing a chance to make the most of his talents. These three, plus Asif Iqbal and Derek Underwood, the good honest yeoman, all put forward a similar argument and Underwood indicated that there had been an inducement for him to break his contract with Packer.

Rewards for players, in established cricket, the message ran, were derisory. The game was badly run. The Cricketers' Association (the players' own body) did little or nothing to further the cause of the players. The Packer intervention would do nothing but good for the game and its participants, not just at Test match level. Ross Edwards from Australia, another excellent but retired Test cricketer, put forward a similar point of view in a most articulate way.

Robert Alexander QC, who led for Packer, had come a long way since he had been Geoffrey Howe's junior at the London Weekend Television case against TCCB back in 1970. This was clearly a case he relished. *Wisdens* were lined up on the table in front of him and he had set out to impress not only the judge with his knowledge of the law and of cricket itself. The court-room was packed every day of the trial and the atmosphere was theatrical, occasionally electric. It gradually became clear, as witness after witness entered the box, that this would not be the seven-day trial we expected.

We had brought over the excellent Ray Steele from Australia, who stayed virtually throughout on a watching brief for the legal actions in Australia, Peter Short from West Indies, M. A. Chidambaram from India, and Walter Hadlee from New Zealand who had sons playing Test cricket. Also acting as witnesses were a number of well-known cricketers from the top level who had not joined Packer, including Geoffrey Boycott and Raymond Illingworth.

As the Packer evidence had unfolded and our witnesses

from ICC member countries had all been questioned with tenacity and at length by Mr Alexander, he had kept hammering home the lack of a contractual position in Test match cricket. It struck me as odd that this should have become an issue, when all the world knew that for individual Test matches one was selected or not by selectors appointed for the purpose. And selection was made from players who were contracted by their counties. Of course he was making the point that those who were not contracted at a particular time were free to enter a contract with another employer, and that the cricket authorities had been penny pinching and parsimonious in not offering contracts for a Test series. This latter point struck me as unfair as one after the other of our witnesses struggled with the question. As day succeeded day, we were obviously having problems in getting across our case for international cricket and the way it was run and the need to keep it intact for the good of all cricket throughout the world. Even the outward appearances of the two parties told different stories. We, the 'medieval barons', lunched on beer and sandwiches in a pub opposite the Law Courts. Kerry Packer, his lawyers and witnesses had a table reserved at the nearby Wig and Pen Club, where the style of living was more generous, the bills infinitely steeper. For some reason, we (pillars of rectitude?) stood in the witness-box, almost as a matter of respect, I suppose. This was in distinct contrast to the opposition.

I had been designated as a sort of ICC sweeper, the fellow to gather together all the arguments for the defence and if necessary add one or two of my own. I felt that somehow we had not given the best possible account of ourselves and responded well, I think, to questions put by Michael Kempster QC acting on behalf of ICC and TCCB. Together we brought out the essential relationships between player and country; the interdependence of country upon country; the way in which the stronger countries helped the weaker ones; in fact the whole *raison d'être* for the International Cricket Conference. It was competitive, yes, but the aim throughout was to help the world

community. The Packer enterprise had creamed off many of
the top players. It was reasonable we should resist in so far as it
was legally possible to do so.

The point was that the vast majority of cricketers throughout
the world would suffer if the game became more fragmented.
The top players were important, but so were the others. There
were no contracts throughout the winter months except for
those on tour. In England, this system enabled players to pursue
other activities, or even claim unemployment benefit, something which they would not be able to do if under a year-round
contract. The trend was set for more money and better rewards
for the top players, but not long ago the whole future of the
game at top level had been in doubt through lack of income.
Only when we were beginning to find our feet did people like
Kerry Packer move in. Theirs was a sheer profit motive; ours,
with amateur committees and a few professionals helping them,
was to preserve and foster the game world wide. It was important to have money to be able to do this, but it wasn't as simple
as a pure profit motive; it would be much simpler if it were.
There was the character and ethos of the game to consider.
There was the whole inter-relationship of country with country
within the commonwealth of cricket to consider.

As for the picture painted of the world's best players being
held in a kind of serfdom, we set out to dispel that image by
pointing to various benefits received, quite beyond any contractual obligation.

The whole question of contracts, or the lack of them, on an
annual basis, had made some of our witnesses stumble through
their evidence, though on the whole they gave an excellent account of themselves, despite being faced with Robert Alexander's formidable presence and somewhat peremptory way of
asking questions.

When counsel for the plaintiff came to ask me one afternoon,
early in my period of cross-examination, whether members of
the ICC believed in a contractual method of employment, again
implying that we behaved like medieval landlords, it struck me

that lawyers asking that question were in a somewhat ambiguous position. They were paid fees, could be changed by their clients at the drop of a hat, were dependent on solicitors for work and solicitors were dependent on casual employment from clients. No sign of any contracts there.

I couldn't resist a gentle counter-attack. Perhaps it was the whole tenseness of the affair. Perhaps it was simply the need to make some sort of positive point in the face of the tidal wave that was moving towards us. Whatever it was, the words, quite unrehearsed, came to mind.

'It is,' I said, with a glance at the mild but straight-faced judge, 'difficult to draw analogies. But – and I mean no disrespect, by what I am about to say – it strikes me that the Test match cricketer and the leading counsel are in much the same boat in terms of contractual employment. For instance, I wonder if you, Mr Alexander, know where your next brief is coming from?'

The pall that hung over the courtroom lifted. There was laughter in court. Spectators, defence counsel and Robert Alexander's own colleagues, even the judge, roared with laughter. It was fun, but it was foolish. I spent another day and a half in the witness box, answering questions from Mr Alexander.

As the world knows, ICC and TCCB lost a case which, by the time all the witnesses had been called and the closing speeches had been made by both sides, and Mr Justice Slade had given his comprehensive and enlightening judgement, had lasted thirty-two days. The cricket authorities had lost on every point of law involved, although they had emerged with some credit from a moral standpoint. Had it all been worth it? Or rather, had we anything to show for the damages and costs awarded against us, amounting to some £250,000 (later shared equally between ICC and TCCB) apart from a vast amount of publicity for cricket all over the world?

Well, for one thing, it had been a lesson. It had taught the cricket authorities that good intentions, if not paving the road to hell, certainly are not enough when it comes to the law of the land. However much of a closed society cricket was, no matter how well the understanding between administrators and players had been in the past, no matter how much of a family atmosphere ran through the game, and no matter how much more the top players had benefited throughout their careers both in terms of money and in so many other ways which would be impossible of definition in contractual terms, there was no point in depending upon loyalty to the system. A contract was a contract and if certain players were required they would have to be issued with legally binding contracts for a twelve-month period or longer.

We also learnt the law regarding inducement to breach of legal contract and what was reasonable in the cricket world, both to protect established cricket and to prevent unlawful restraint of trade.

As John Arlott said at the time, 'It [cricket] will never be the same again'. Recent events in Pakistan and elsewhere have borne out, only too well, what can happen when a thoroughly professional game of such complexity as cricket becomes, through its financial aspects, temporarily divorced from the game which is played for enjoyment by millions throughout the world.

Back in 1977, however, the world of cricket was faced with a dire dilemma. As far as Test match cricket was concerned, players who were signed by Packer were initially unavailable, and that was that. During the case, and at a comparatively early stage, our counsel had entered a defence that ICC and TCCB were employers' associations and as such immune, as were trade unions under current law, from the charges brought against them. The rules and prime activities of both bodies were not held to constitute them as employers' associations, but almost as soon as the case was over TCCB set about amending their rules and constitution to enable them so to qualify.

So the determination of those responsible for 'authorized' cricket to continue to protect the interests of the game they cherished went on. A battle was still being waged, on the field and off, but now it was a case of letting the 'devil take the hindmost'

1. A fine piece of real estate.
Lord's Cricket Ground seen from an airship in 1987.
The new Mound stand is in place and the bicentenary match in progress.

2. The Essex team, 1954. *Back row, left to right:* Les Savill, Ken Preston, Bill Greensmith, Dick Horsfall, Dickie Dodds, Paul Gibb; *front row, left to right:* Frank Vigar, Trevor Bailey, Doug Insole, Ray Smith, the author.

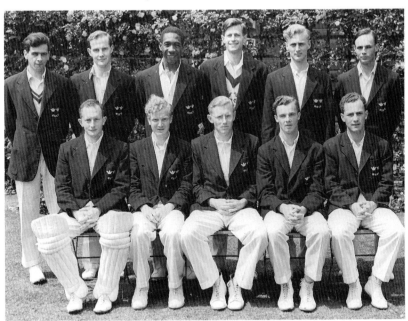

3. Oxford University, 1956. *Back row, left to right:* S. V. M. Clube, S. G. Metcalfe, E. S. M. Kentish, the author, I. M. Gibson, M. A. Eagar; *front row, left to right:* A. P. Walshe, J. M. Allan, M. J. K. Smith, A. C. Walton, G. P. S. Delisle.

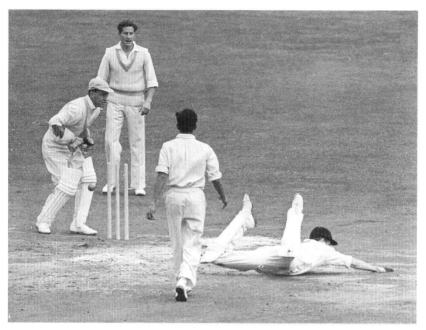

4. Oxford v. Cambridge, Lord's, 1956. The author ends up in a thoroughly undignified position but in time to prevent M. E. L. Melluish running him out, while J. F. Pretlove and G. Goonasena look on.

5. En route for East Africa, 1957: MCC board the plane.
From the front: F. R. Brown (captain) (Cambridge University, Northamptonshire and England), S. C. Griffith (Sussex and England), P. E. Richardson (Worcestershire, Kent and England), G. H. G. Doggart (Cambridge University, Sussex and England), R. V. C. Robins (Middlesex), A. C. D. Ingleby-Mackenzie (Hampshire), M. J. K. Smith (Oxford University, Warwickshire and England), J. J. Warr (Cambridge University, Middlesex and England), C. J. M. Kenny (Cambridge University and Essex), D. R. W. Silk (Cambridge University and Somerset), the author, G. W. Cook (Cambridge University).

6. The crowd outside the Grace Gates at Lord's, having left the ground after a bomb warning during the England v. West Indies Test in 1973 . . .

7. . . . but one MCC member clearly cannot understand what all the fuss is about.

8. Ray Illingworth holds up the Benson & Hedges Cup after the final
at Lord's in 1974, in which Leicestershire defeated Middlesex.
Ted Dexter, Cecil Paris, the MCC President, and the author
are to the left of the presentation party.

9. The teams taking part in the inaugural World Cup pictured at Lord's
in 1975 before the competition began. *Left to right*: Wales,
East Africa, Argentina, Bangladesh, Holland, Fiji, Sri Lanka, Pakistan,
West Indies, England, Australia, New Zealand, India, Canada,
Singapore, Bermuda, Malaysia, Papua New Guinea.

10. The World Cup, 1975. After receiving the trophy from the Duke of Edinburgh, President of MCC, Clive Lloyd has time to examine the cheque, presented by the Prudential to the winners.

11. Tony Greig and Kerry Packer leave the Law Courts after the first day of a long, long, hearing. Already they appeared confident of the outcome.

12. The MCC Committee in session, 1978. D. G. Clark, the President, is in the chair. To his left sit the author, G. C. K. Rowe (Assistant Secretary), G. O. Allen, J. S. O. Haslewood, R. V. C. Robins, F. W. Millett and E. W. Swanton. On the President's right sit J. G. W. Davies, E. W. Phillips, V. J. Lawrence (Assistant Secretary), Lord Caccia, R. Aird, C. G. A. Paris, O. J. Wait and C. N. Cosh. On the inside of the table, *from the front and left to right*, sit C. J. Harrison, F. G. Mann, S. C. Griffith, G. C. Newman, M. G. Crawford, W. H. Webster and Sir Cyril Hawker.

13. The Centenary Test match, England v. Australia, Lord's, 1980. A match bedevilled by mishaps but a memorable gathering of the clans.

14. The Queen and Max Walker, England v. Australia, Lord's, 1975.
The others in the picture, *from left to right*, are Dennis Lillee, Doug Walters,
Ian Chappell, the author and G. O. Allen.

15. The Queen at Lord's shaking hands with David Gower, the England captain,
during the England v. Australia Test in 1985. The officials in the picture are,
from left to right, the author, David Clark, Treasurer of MCC,
and F. G. Mann, President of MCC.

by proving which form of cricket was the best. Australia during the coming winter was to be the first battleground. Australia v. India on the one hand, the Packer circus on the other.

There was no doubt in the minds of many current players and virtually all the great players of the past that everything should be done to discourage Packer and his 'gimmickry' which, in their view, was a corruption of the game. Among other things this was to lead to a proliferation of tours and Test matches throughout the world. We had to play to be able to pay the players; they had to play to earn their pay.

For the future, on the part of international cricket, two fundamental aims were established by the Chairman and the Secretary. It was vital to capitalize on the degree of unity which had been formed in adversity among the members of ICC. And it was essential to give every possible support to our friends in Australia. Sooner rather than later Packer had to come to terms with us and we with him. Any rapprochement would be best achieved if we were in a position of strength and speaking with one voice. A considerable part of my time during the next couple of years was to be devoted to the furtherance of these two objectives.

Those strange, alien days in court had their full share of off-beat moments, apart from the series of conferences in counsel's chambers and the unusual sequence of highs and lows we passed through from day to day, as the case seemed to fluctuate first one way, then the other.

There was the moment of meeting Walter Hadlee at London Airport. He had been speedy beyond the call of duty in answering the call to attend as a witness. He had jumped on practically the first possible aircraft to be with us, had travelled virtually non-stop half way round the world and he had found himself dead tired and disorientated at Heathrow in the still hours of the early morning, *sans* luggage – it had been off-loaded in San Francisco – and, for all he knew, stranded. I had driven out to meet him, something he hadn't expected, and the relief on his face and the feeling with which he exclaimed, 'Jack, I've never been so glad to see anyone in my life!' was as moving as it was gratifying, coming from one of the great men of cricket at three o'clock in the morning.

There was the conversation with Amit Roy, the *Daily Telegraph* correspondent. We were talking over the pros and cons of the case at quite an early stage of the proceedings. Amit Roy was close to the Indian Board of Control and we were discussing reactions to Packer in India.

'The general population are mostly ignorant about the implications,' he said, 'but they and the Indian Board are very upset by what has happened so far.'

'I think that's true of all those running cricket throughout the world,' I said.

'Yes, but with our people it's different. They are extremely cross with Packer because he has signed players from nearly every Test match country except India. Not one Indian has he chosen. What's wrong with our players?'

There was the first morning of the case. Ray Steele, Walter Hadlee, Donald Carr and I had arranged to meet at Lord's and go by a taxi previously ordered. The taxi didn't turn up. Eventually, four large men crammed into a mini driven by Sally Pollott, my secretary, arriving just in time, distinctly crumpled, but having had a most useful meeting between bumps along the way.

There was the moment when, after about the fifteenth day of the trial, with no ending in sight, I was trapped in a lift in the Law Courts. The other occupants were Ian Johnson, former captain of Australia, and Alex Bannister of the *Daily Mail*. In order to remove our minds from the claustrophobic effects, knowing we had at least half-an-hour to wait before the repair man arrived, we talked inconsequentially. I recounted how I had gone, with Ray Steele and Walter Hadlee, to the Wig and Pen Club across the road the previous evening to meet Denis Compton and Colin Ingleby-Mackenzie for a drink after the day's proceedings. Naturally, being non-members, we had waited for our hosts to arrive. To remedy the situation for any future occasion, Ingleby disappeared into the Secretary's office and emerged with a membership card for me. Not just a membership, but a Life Membership. Standing there in the lift we pondered, why the *Life* Membership? We concluded that all pointers were in favour of the Wig and Pen having the feeling that the case was going to last a very long time. Or was it that they knew about the Law Court lifts and hadn't given me very long anyway?

There was the moment in court when Ray Steele was asked by counsel for the plaintiffs whether he thought the Packer contracts with his players were legal and enforceable.

'I do not doubt it,' said Ray. 'There's a saying in Australia that the only way out of a Packer contract is by becoming pregnant. I don't suppose that applies to many of our cricketers.'

Laughter in court. But . . .

The Packer case made a profound impression on me. More than ever, I could see the need for a strong independent MCC, a case for a growing role as an honest broker. If we were to fulfil that task as we should, it kept coming back to me, then we must at all costs retain control of Lord's. The events of the past year or so had given me little cause to doubt that we would.

But I had reckoned without the small clouds yet to gather in the shape of the 1980 Centenary Test match.

6

PICKING UP THE PIECES

THE RAMIFICATIONS OF Kerry Packer's intervention and the continuous problems presented by the plight of South African cricketers – of all races – remained at the forefront of my activities on behalf of the International Cricket Conference. By the time the court case was ended, MCC had a new President in David Clark and consequently ICC had a new Chairman.

One of our first ventures in a new partnership was to embark on a trip around the world. The aim was to visit all the Test playing countries in turn, pass on to them the advice we had taken about the advisability of appealing against the judgement on Packer, and, above all, to seek a thread of consistency among the various countries as to how the Packer threat should be dealt with. There was also the question of £250,000 which would shortly be required and we wanted to be sure that the countries involved would be willing to pay up. It was a rapid trip: around the world in fifteen days.

In Lahore we met the England team. Difficult moments were

being experienced. Talk of flying back two or three Pakistan players from Australia, where they were with the Packer outfit, was rife. The England players were not too happy about the air of uncertainty that had been created. The Pakistan Board was split on the question of Packer players. David Clark had managed several tours abroad, and was well skilled in dealing with the Pakistan temperament. During the two days or so that we were there he performed wonders. We spoke reassuringly to the England players under Mike Brearley at the invitation of Ken Barrington the manager, and had a successful meeting with the Pakistan Board of Control, who had problems with their own players and with some of their own members.

The President of Pakistan himself was, eventually to relieve them of some of the pressures they were under to play Packer players in the Test matches against England by saying no. But at that time, we had the assurances of the Pakistan Board that they had no intention of selecting players who were not wholly committed to them, although they did not themselves really know which way the cat would jump. Convinced of the good will of the majority and armed with the agreement that Pakistan would pay their share of the court case costs, and that no appeal should be made, we embarked for India and Bangalore (a marvellous place).

The Indian authorities made a special fuss of us. They could not have been kinder or more helpful. Both our chief missions were accomplished with the minimum of fuss. No appeal; yes, they would pay their share. There was no question of any of their boys going to Packer. Not now.

In Melbourne, where we met the Australian Board and saw a glimpse of the Test match against India, we were in the front line. The atmosphere almost held a whiff of cordite. All the talk was of beating Packer. There was no question over the determination of Bob Parish and his colleagues. The courts constituted one battleground, the matches held in direct opposition by Packer's WSC and the Australian Board and televised on rival channels were another. It seemed then that if any member of the International Cricket Conference might stand in the way of an eventual settlement, it would be Australia. At that time there was a Churchillian mood about them.

Sadly, we could spend only one day in New Zealand: Melbourne, Christchurch, Auckland and a Pan Am flight to Los Angeles on the same day. There was nothing but total support from Walter Hadlee and his colleagues. New Zealand like India had not been affected by the loss of players to Packer, but they were staunch in their support of Australia and of the ICC line. No appeal; no surrender.

There was an underlying urgency about our journey round the world. We had to give notice within a certain time of the High Court verdict if an appeal was to be lodged, and there was, besides, much to be done before a special meeting of ICC to be held on 1 February. There was little chance to sleep on the chaotic non-stop Pan Am flight from Auckland to Los Angeles, but at least we had a room booked at the other end where five or six hours sleep would be possible before taking the next plane to Port of Spain, Trinidad.

We had just checked into our hotel when the telephone rang. The United States Cricket Association, having been alerted by John Gardner, their representative in the UK, had formed a small welcoming party and would like to come round. I wanted desperately to make some excuse, but under David Clark's watchful and unrelenting eye, I was powerless. Quite rightly, he insisted that we should be hospitable; and, quite rightly, we were. I only hope to this day we did not give away how exhausted we felt and that we made some sort of sense when talking over drinks and sandwiches while two or three hours ticked by and the tremendous enthusiasm of those men who keep cricket flourishing in the United States washed over us.

And so to Trinidad where an altogether different set of problems faced us. It was evident that the West Indies administrators, great cricketers with a sense of the game's traditions, were up against it. The West Indies team had been signed *en masse* by Packer. Some members of the West Indies Board were against opposing him. The people of the islands, whose heroes had their blessing in earning as much money as they could from whatever source, were keen that they should play in Test matches for West Indies as well as for Packer, and they felt they had no choice but to select their best team for the series against Australia. That the players, led by their captain, Clive Lloyd, were eventually to walk out on the Board, before the Guyana Test match, was ironical. The incident occurred, we learned later, because one of the Packer players had been left out of the team, with West Indies two up in the series. Again later, suspicions were voiced that the West Indies players had Mr Packer's full backing in this destructive act. By *force majeur*, the West Indies were destined to build a new team.

But all this happened before our meeting. We left for England in the knowledge that it might be a long time before the West Indies could meet the costs of the court case, that they were certainly against any possibility of an appeal and that they had problems, through no fault of the administrators, which were peculiarly and particularly difficult. They were bound to be a weak link in the chain.

Back in London the special ICC meeting on 1 February agreed that there should be no appeal. David Clark and I were appointed to be ICC's representatives in negotiations with Packer until an agreement was reached which was acceptable to all Test playing countries. This meant that David might well have to go beyond his one-year term of office. In fact, of course, he did.

It was also apparent then, and during the following few months, that certain TCCB noses had been put out of joint by the way MCC, through its running of ICC, was gaining too much kudos and publicity. What could and should have been a period of all quiet on the Lord's front, was anything but. As a Test match ground Lord's and MCC were subjected to severe pressure to surrender their authority in various ways.

David Clark and I were nominated as sole negotiators by the

ICC. It had been agreed by the ICC that individual countries would not deal with Packer's organization. Of course, the Packer organization then did their best to peel off the member countries one by one and had come close to achieving this to some degree in Pakistan and in the West Indies.

As time went by, however, there was little doubt that, for all the incredible ability of the organization set up by World Series Cricket to overcome their political problems, and for all their seemingly inexhaustible supply of money and their well-oiled public relations machine, real success in cricket terms could only come in Australia. Even there, real success was unlikely if this meant taking over from authorized cricket. Packer had overcome the obstacles of certain Test match grounds being unavailable to him, he had introduced day/night cricket which did capture the Australian public and he had certainly hit the Australian Cricket Board where it hurt, chiefly in the pocket but also in the way he had overcome seemingly unsurmountable obstacles.

Of great concern in the general sense, was what was happening within the control of World Series Cricket to the traditional and time-tested aspects of the game, which for cricket followers were a precious part of their heritage. Cricket with World Series Cricket was presented as a battle of the gladiators. The hype was concerned with the dangerous elements of the game: the helmet, the bouncer, the slog; not much here about the charm of cricket.

With the progress of day/night, limited-overs cricket during Packer's second season, and the young, Packer-emasculated Australian team receiving a sound beating in the Ashes series, and the seemingly interminable round of court cases, it was evident that the Australian Cricket Board were bleeding. They were not mortally wounded, but they had been hurt.

David Clark and I had initiated another meeting with Packer representatives in June of 1978. The meeting took place in the Pierre Hotel, New York. The venue was chosen chiefly to fit in with their travelling plans, and it had the added advantage of being one place where confidentiality could virtually be guaranteed. It was a quick turnround for us and largely a water-testing operation for both sides. Andrew Caro and Lynton Taylor, the World Series Cricket envoys, made a case which, involving as it did clashes with nearly all organized tours and Test match programmes, proved impossible for us to recommend to ICC and it was eventually rejected unanimously by them. The strong impression left with us was that no real attempt had been made to come to terms.

Again, during the Australian summer of 1979 we arranged a meeting in Sydney, this time in company with Charles Palmer, by then Chairman of ICC and President of MCC. The meeting was held against the background of a World Series tour of the West Indies, which made it seem that Packer's intrusion into the cricket world would be more permanent than was originally supposed. There had also been ructions in domestic English cricket, where the Cricketers' Association had been advocating an attitude different from the county clubs which had embraced Packer players in their bids for success in the English season. David Clark had felt bound to resign from Kent, with whom over the years he had become virtually synonymous, as a result. He consulted me before he did so. With the best will in the world I found it difficult to dissuade him, since in his role for world cricket as an honest broker, he felt strongly that being associated with Kent's currently parochial attitude would compromise his efforts.

The Sydney meeting was enlightening in several respects. We had not sat round a table with Packer himself before this, apart from at that fateful meeting at Lord's. I had exchanged pleasantries with him during the London court case, but that was all. We had come with an open mind, willing to listen, anxious to discuss whether there was any common ground between the views of the Australian Board and what Packer would be prepared to accept or vice versa. It was in all our minds that here was the real battleground. It was also a meeting held without a brief from ICC members, although we knew that some of them, notably West Indies for their own understandable reasons, would be in favour of peace at almost any price. A civilized atmosphere prevailed throughout. Packer's team was a strong one: Cornell of PBL, the marketing arm of World Series Cricket, Packer himself, Lynton Taylor and Packer's financial director. There was little question now of the swagger which had been present at Lord's in June 1979. There was no attitude spelling out that 'devil take the hindmost' was the dominant mood prevailing.

I came away with two main insistent thoughts running through my mind. One was that Packer would come to a deal and disband his own operation if he was granted world television rights; although he would try immensely hard to gain a lot more than that, by seeking to control what fare was served up on his channel. The second, I brushed aside as being the result of an over-suspicious nature. Yet it kept on returning like a still, small voice. It insisted that the Australian Board had already had some form of dialogue with Packer, despite the insistence world-wide that the three of us would be sole negotiators. It seemed relatively unimportant in the overall scheme of things anyway, and the possibility was never mentioned in our subsequent discussions with the Australians. We flew off round the world, once again, to report the results of our discussions and to seek the views of the Test playing countries.

Almost immediately after our return to England, Charles Palmer and I, again in our capacities as ICC Chairman and Secretary, embarked on another delicate journey: a fact-finding mission to South Africa in company with members of a number of ICC countries. We had had little respite from international affairs that year, and the South African Cricket Union had been constantly knocking on our door, with good reason in terms of all *they* had managed to achieve. But although I eventually submitted a long, relatively favourable, and certainly accurate report as a result of that visit, the ICC as a whole would have none of it.

It seemed undeniable now that South Africa was out on a

limb until the laws of that country were changed. It was no longer a matter of multi-racial cricket and selection on merit. The time spent in South Africa had been a significant coming together of the nations in another respect. Bob Parish, the Australian Chairman, was present throughout, and it was during our time in South Africa, which lasted two weeks or so, that it was unofficially established, during various off-the-record meetings, that the Australian Cricket Board could talk on a one-to-one basis with Packer's outfit and report back on progress to the ICC in London. Since so much depended on the televising of cricket in Australia it seemed that the only real prospect of reaching a permanent solution lay with those hitherto implacable foes meeting face to face with the blessing of ICC. It is fair to say that a more conciliatory stance was not discouraged, but some of what happened during the next month or two came like a bolt from the blue.

Only weeks after our return from South Africa I was astonished to learn that a deal had been struck between these two previously bitter adversaries. There had been no attempt to keep the ICC in the picture. Actually, now that there was no other obligations standing in the way, the granting of television rights to Packer's Channel 9 for a three-year period, at a greatly increased fee for the Australian Board, was a relief. Moreover, it seemed altogether sensible as it was bound to bring about the demise of World Series Cricket. Even Packer would not want two lots of cricket matches on his screens.

However, to grant TV rights to Packer was one thing. The extent of Australian Board's apparent commitment to him and the complete upheaval of the pattern of Australian and, by implication, world cricket was quite another.

I read the telex from Bob Parish giving me details of the agreement with surprise and foreboding. As the full implications sunk in, these emotions were supplanted by bewilderment. Talking to Bob Parish on the telephone did little to assuage my sense of disappointment. As far as I could make out, reading between the lines, Australian cricket was effectively to be run for the benefit of Packer's Channel 9, with one of Packer's companies calling all the shots. Was it to be cricket in Australia which was televised by Channel 9, or was it to be a series of scheduled TV programmes into which cricket in terms of its format and its whole ambience was expected to fit?

The agreement contained the following clauses, among others:

'The Board has granted PBL Sports Pty Ltd the exclusive right, for a term of ten years, to promote the programme of cricket organized by the Board and to arrange the televising and merchandizing in respect of that programme. For the first three years of the agreement the Board has agreed that PBL Sports Pty Ltd may arrange a contract for the televising of the programme with the Channel 9 network.

It is envisaged that the programme each season will comprise five or six Test matches and an international one-day series, to be known as the Benson and Hedges World Series Cup, of fifteen matches plus a final which will be the best of five matches. These international matches will involve two overseas teams and the Australian team. The programme will also include the Sheffield Shield competition and a one-day series of nine matches between the states.

Playing conditions of all matches will be under the control of the Board and the Board has agreed to consider favourably the introduction of the 30-yard circle in limited-overs matches, day/night matches and, on an experimental basis, the use of coloured clothing in Benson and Hedges one-day limited-overs international matches.

The programme for the 1979–80 season will not be finally determined for some weeks. England and India have accepted invitations to come to Australia in 1979–80. The Board has agreed to ask the Indian board to defer their visit until next season, 1980–81, and will invite the West Indian Board to send an official team to participate in the 1979–80 programme.

The Board is unanimously of the opinion that its decision to accept the proposal from PBL is in the best interests of Australian and international cricket.'

It was hard to avoid the sense of being hijacked twice in a couple of years: first by Packer and now by the Australian Cricket Board.

But there was never any real doubt that the deal would be accepted – as it had to be. It would be up to individual countries to strike the best deals they could with the Australian authorities who were only bound to use their best endeavours when it came to programming; although there was comparatively little that could be done in reality.

The Indians, kind souls, were mollified by an offer to tour the following year. We never found out the financial terms which had been finally settled between Packer and the Australian Board. Some felt rather let down. World cricket had rallied behind Australia in her hour of need. Everyone had been badly affected financially and in other ways by the giving of that support. Without consultation, they had been pushed into an alien world, which they mistrusted and, as far as we could see, Australian cricket was unable, or unwilling, to offer any form of recompense. This was an unfair view, considering the plight of the Australian Cricket Board. But the refusal of the Australian authorities to reveal the financial aspects of their agreement with PBL, while seeking the full co-operation of the rest of world cricket to a programme many of them disliked on sight, ruffled more than a few feathers.

What had previously been despised was now apparently to be warmly received by all concerned. The moulding of the Australian season to fit the needs of a television station was one aspect which went against the grain. The marketing techniques which played (successfully) on some of the more dubious aspects of the game was another. The intrusion of television into many areas previously the province of the players, or the umpires, or the administrators was difficult to accept. Above all there was the immediate feeling that the television tail was now wagging the Australian cricket dog and hence the international kennel.

After an initial settling down period, it had to be accepted that Bob Parish and his colleagues on the Australian Board had had to solve the problem as best they could. We all had to make the best of it.

Adjustments to the programme have been insisted on in recent years by some visiting countries with the outcome of preserving the five-day Test match as the pinnacle of what the game has to offer. But there is now too much cricket, especially one-day cricket, being played on the international circuit; first, as a direct result of Packer's intervention; now, because the profit motive appears to demand it.

The effect of all this on standards of behaviour has been unwelcome, and the use of intrusive television techniques serves only to highlight all kinds of extravagant behaviour.

The advent of Channel 9 had produced, in terms of sheer television coverage, a technical revolution, which other companies operating where cricket is played have not been slow to evaluate. Excellence of coverage is one thing. However, microphones in places on the field of play where every sound is transferred into the homes of those watching are both unnecessary and unfair to the average player, if his every word can be heard, as in Pakistan in 1987–88, and later in New Zealand.

Running almost step by step with the problems presented on the international front by World Series Cricket had been the shadow of South African cricket. The South African Cricket Union had come out in favour of ICC during the Packer controversy, their whole approach having been in favour of established cricket of which they still felt and, in the eyes of many still were, a part. With the co-operation of successive chairmen, the South African issue had been kept before the ICC. The South African cricketers had done all that had been asked of them, following the cancellation of the 1970 tour, and deserved every chance of putting their case to the governing body of world cricket. The days of sweeping such issues under the carpet were long gone.

It was of course naïve to suppose that those cricketing countries directly under the political control of their governments, which included the vast majority of those represented on the ICC, would or could consent to the continuance of tours by any member country until the apartheid laws were changed. It was a message we had continually to convey to Rashid Verachia, the President of SACU, Joe Parmensky, Geoff Dakin and others. The visit of a delegation to South Africa in 1979 had given a brief glimpse of hope that ICC would be able to make some move in the direction of their avowed intent of fostering cricket wherever it is played, but the meeting of the ICC which followed the report, endorsed by all representatives who had visited South Africa, soon knocked any such hope on the head. The report was rejected out of hand. It was not even 'received' officially by the Conference.

So, four years after the Packer upheaval, in 1982, countries were faced with another type of defection from authorized cricket: the South African rebels were born. It was, like Packer's, a cleverly clandestine operation. I was in Colombo for the inaugural Test match between Sri Lanka and England, and, apart from a feeling that things weren't quite as normal – certain players appeared concerned and worried, almost as if they were looking for someone to take into their confidence – no inkling of the imminent departure for South Africa of Graham Gooch and his team reached me.

With the escalation of such rebel tours to South Africa – with Sri Lankans following Englishmen, the West Indians following them, and then the Australians – went the last faint chance, if one there had ever been, of being able to welcome multi-racial South African cricket back into the international scene. Blacklists drawn up on behalf of a United Nations subcommittee and the actions of various Commonwealth governments have since been instrumental in outlawing players who go to South Africa, even for coaching purposes, from playing in international cricket in certain countries.

Throughout this whole period, everyone administering cricket from Lord's was generally too taken up with the wide public issues – Packer, South Africa, and the like – to be overwhelmingly concerned with altering the status quo at headquarters, however desirable that might be.

It is possible to understand the problems that MCC's patronage sometimes presented to the TCCB, Middlesex and others living at Lord's, but there seemed to me to be only one way the place could be run and this view merely followed that of the MCC Committee during those years. True, there were those such as George Mann, Doug Insole and from time to time others whose natural power base was the TCCB, but who according to the custom sat from time to time on the MCC Committee, who saw things differently. If it was possible to accommodate certain proposals such as greater entertainment facilities during big matches to both TCCB and the sponsors and others, then they were being accommodated.

We went along with the TCCB proposal that Peter Lush should fulfil a press relations function at Lord's during the big matches, although it was also agreed that this could only work satisfactorily if there was the closest possible liaison between me, acting on behalf of MCC, and him.

Other small but important areas of a sensitive nature were also examined, and if friction was not avoided, it was kept to a sustainable minimum.

The high profile given to MCC through its President and Secretary during the continuously troubled times of the mid-1970s, I believe, made those responsible within the TCCB for the overall organization of the game in England feel threatened. It was perhaps a natural reaction to the continuing influence, at least in the eyes of the world, of MCC which remained very much in the centre of world affairs, though it had given up the right to control the game in England.

Now, as MCC's high profile on the international scene faded from view, efforts to push the Club right into the background became more blatant – despite the fact that the work being done on behalf of international cricket lost none of its importance and despite the fact that MCC, through Lord's, continued to pull more than its weight financially on the national scene.

A three-man committee, with Raman Subba Row in the chair, sought to remove MCC, apart from one vote, from the game's governing body. This proposal also advocated the removal of the Cricket Council in favour of a new Board, controlled by the professional game. This was not accepted by the counties themselves, who continued to support the two-tier system of the Cricket Council with TCCB as one of its constituents. But the counties' support availed MCC little. In no time, the advocacy of George Mann, Doug Insole and others had brought about a revised constitution for the Cricket Council which seriously reduced MCC's participation and gave TCCB an overall majority and the chairmanship. It also invested TCCB with most of the Cricket Council's previous powers on an irrevocable basis.

One thing followed another. MCC's membership of TCCB could have cost them financially dear if various attempts at TCCB level to reduce the Club's income or to lay hands on various sources of income historically and currently available to the Club through its own efforts, had not been resisted by the MCC Committee who saw the dangerous trend events were taking. With George Mann in the chair of both TCCB and Middlesex and on the MCC Committee, MCC's stalwarts were placed in an unenviable position.

By 1980, I was in the position of reflecting that despite dealing with Packer and the attendant problems, and even through all the South African saga, I had positively enjoyed my work. By comparison, protecting the reasonable interests of MCC and its members was a burden. Retaining control of Lord's exercised me and my colleagues and, inevitably, the MCC Committee, more than I had remotely imagined they would. The efforts made by MCC on behalf of the international community had earned us respect but in an odd way had made us more envied in our own country.

The position in the early eighties was summed up pretty accurately in Geoffrey Moorhouse's excellent book on Lord's, written recently enough to bear witness to the struggles going on at this time. He recognized the emerging influence of the 'young buffers', Bernard Coleman and Raman Subba Row, and also of the cricket men such as Doug Insole and George Mann. Doug Insole is described as having been somewhere close to the levers of power in either TCCB or MCC or both since 1963. A similar position is ascribed to George Mann, Chairman of the TCCB from 1978 to 1983 and on the MCC Committee pretty well throughout. He describes Mann as 'in many ways the oddest figure who could possibly be found to head any organization seeking to demote the Marylebone Cricket Club. A deceptively languid character with a taste for monogrammed shirts. . . .' Mann of course came from a cricketing family, had played for Eton, Cambridge and Middlesex, and had captained England with success.

'The thoroughly baffling thing,' Moorhouse concludes, 'about all the wrangles that took place up to the reconstitution of the Cricket Council in 1983, is that hardly any differences of opinion exist between the MCC Committee and the TCCB executive on major issues affecting the conduct and playing of cricket. They share the same stance on a whole range of matters . . . So frequently are individuals to be found with one foot planted firmly in each camp, that it is rather difficult to avoid the suspicion that the long debate has not really been about the ideal structure of administration at all. It may have been about that primitive pastime of human beings when power is at stake: jostling each other to determine who shall enjoy the greater share. Something of the sort happened once before, nearly 200 years ago, when the arrivistes of Marylebone shouldered aside the old guard from Hambledon.'

Some pretty fierce jostling was going on now all right, and, as a defender of the faith, I was right in the middle.

7

SOME PROGRESS, SOME
PROBLEMS

ALTHOUGH WE WERE by no means out of the wood on the international front, the early 1980s produced more opportunities to reflect on the advantages there were in being Secretary of MCC. To work for something you believed in; to be surrounded by friends from way back, from home and overseas; to be at the centre of world cricket, if only marginally involved in the running of UK cricket. And above all, Lord's.

I would sometimes look back to see what had been achieved since 1974, apart from holding on to the integrity of the Club and keeping faith with the needs of cricket and of the membership. It was sometimes difficult to separate the accidental or incidental from the deliberately achieved, but certain things came to mind.

Without departing from the tough basic principles of election to a private members' club, MCC now stood at an all-time high in terms of desirability. After increasing membership from 16,000 to 18,000 the waiting list had become negligible, but now it had grown again so that there was a nominal thirty years between proposal and election. Cricket, real tennis and squash were thriving. The Club had retained both its international flavour and its essential nature as a club for cricketers. A large building maintenance programme was in train; the fabric of the Club was being cared for. The indoor cricket school had been built and was thriving, thanks to the thrust provided by Jim Swanton and John Haslewood. The playing staff, which it had once been proposed should be cut drastically, was fulfilling, more than ever before, its function as a nursery for well trained professional cricketers. The Club was financially sound, both from the point of view of assets and liquid funds, though I had been on the losing side in trying to prevent the sale of certain of its freehold properties. Equally important, the staff were relatively well paid and taking a pride in their job. There had been a time when the privilege of working at Lord's had been an inordinately large part of the reward of those employed by MCC. Now, at least, loyal service was better rewarded financially and working conditions had been improved. David Clark, Ted Phillips and Sir Anthony Tuke had all been supportive in that area.

It seemed likely, too, that more and more people had come to appreciate the efforts made on behalf of world cricket, not merely by providing the Chairman and Secretary of ICC., or by the work done quietly and continuously behind the scenes, but by virtue of an acknowledgement of MCC's independence.

On the other side of the coin had been the disappointing occasion of the Centenary Test match, when the weather and the well meaning but sometimes chaotic running of the match jointly by MCC and TCCB had sounded warning bells in my ears against any such repetition. Another setback had been the rowdy behaviour of some MCC members on that occasion which had done the Club no good at all.

In 1982 some of the members, during a couple of meetings, had made it clear to the Committee that they were not happy with the way the Club was being run. There were complaints about the way the Committee was elected, its distance from the membership, its preoccupation with the interests of other bodies outside the membership, and they made some telling points about the way the membership had been neglected. It was the opinion of many that the position of MCC's membership at Lord's should be advanced, rather than continually eroded to the benefit of other bodies with whom they, as members, had no connection. The small remuneration the club received from matches staged at Lord's was also questioned, as was the age of some of those serving on the Committee.

The Committee then agreed that an internal working-party should be set up consisting of four members of the Committee and four other members of the Club with distinguished backgrounds. The Treasurer, David Clark, was in the chair, with Nick Cosh (the finance director of a city company), Oliver Popplewell QC, Robin Sligh (the managing director of Seckers) and Ted Clark (a former Middlesex cricketer) from the Committee. The other members were Michael Sissons (a distinguished literary agent), Charles Fry (Chairman of a highly successful City enterprise), Robin Leigh-Pemberton (later to become Governor of the Bank of England) and Alex Bennett (formerly Chairman of Whitbread).

Eventually, after many meetings, an interim report, put to the members in April 1983, included in its recommendations the installation of properly conducted financial negotiations with TCCB regarding the future use of Lord's for Test and other major matches. This interim report was accepted by the Committee as a whole, though influential individuals on the Committee had expressed reservations about two particular aspects – a recommendation that an age limit of seventy should be placed upon members of the Committee, and that very careful consideration should be given to revising the system whereby representatives of other cricketing bodies were almost inevitably asked to serve on the MCC Committee. However, there was support from the Committee for the vast bulk of this interim report, including sections which supported MCC's responsibility for what happened at Lord's at all times and the right of members to enter Lord's without payment being made beyond their subscription, and both sections were included in the final report.

Only the 'seventy rule' was represented to the members as being toned down by allowing room for election to the Committee, or other designated posts, after the age of seventy in exceptional circumstances. The final report, approved by the Committee and endorsed by the membership at the Annual General Meeting in May 1984, was a statement of policy and intent.

Indeed the intention to get matters onto a different footing had been signalled to those members influential within TCCB and sitting on the MCC Committee early in 1983, when the interim report was under discussion. The TCCB hierarchy were officially informed, in any case, of the way MCC intended to proceed. The TCCB Executive Committee, or someone acting on their behalf, was quick off the mark with a response. On 23 July a document entitled 'Discussion Paper' was sent to all Test match grounds. Its intention was clear. It aimed to lump MCC in with all other grounds under the canopy of TCCB's right to intervene or interfere in all arrangements made for any Test match (or by the same token, any county match) as and when it chose to do so. The clear message was that if TCCB wanted extra facilities, no matter what, they should be given. The possibility of payment for these was mentioned, but the right of proper negotiations was not. Maximum delegation to the executive of the grounds concerned was indicated, but the right of TCCB to prevail was spelled out clearly.

MCC had been constrained to point out deficiencies in a system which claimed all grounds were the same, but which took from MCC and its members substantially more financially and in the way of facilities than from any other ground. Not only was this true match for match, but in terms of big matches in general MCC alone contributed considerably more to the TCCB pool than it received from the eventual distribution of profits.

MCC were pleased in every way to provide more. But they wanted a say in how much more. Furthermore, MCC were geographically placed in an invidious position. The TCCB lived there. They were present at all matches played at Lord's, before, during and after. Other grounds, rarely visited by anyone in authority, could by and large agree to any delegation of powers without fear of implementation; MCC, though, might only be left sweeping out the pavilion and getting everything ready for the TCCB to take over.

At this stage in 1983 George Mann emerged significantly as wearing more hats than could comfortably be fitted on anyone's head. He was Chairman of the TCCB and of the Cricket Council and part author of the TCCB's 'Discussion Paper'. He was President and Chairman of Middlesex. He sat on the MCC Committee, and the then President of MCC, Sir Anthony Tuke, was a great personal friend and set great store by what Mann said.

With all this in mind, and with the advocacy of Oliver Popplewell QC at the helm of those in favour of resistance to any measure which hit at the heart of the principles under which the Club operated, the MCC Committee had been faced with an intensely difficult decision over a new levy to be placed on members attending World Cup matches. After much heart-searching the Committee had previously agreed to stump up a considerable sum to TCCB as payment for members attending Test matches. Now the imposition of a further levy for the third World Cup of 1983 was seen by many to be the last straw.

Although the members of MCC could be kept in the dark about this if the money were obtained from Club funds, it would involve an unwarranted last-minute adjustment to the financial conditions of the World Cup. Neither MCC, nor any other ground due to stage World Cup matches, had been able to argue the matter at a properly convened meeting, and as Secretary of the International Cricket Conference, which had overall responsibility for the competition, I was conscious of no decision by ICC which would permit this. In spite of a strong recommendation to the contrary by the sub-committee, of which Oliver Popplewell was Chairman, the Committee agreed to pay the levy.

Even so, the MCC Committee was at that time conscious of their obligations to the membership and determined on proper negotiations. The TCCB discussion paper was not accepted as a basis for future policy. As Oliver Popplewell had already proposed, and the Committee had accepted, MCC should put together a comprehensive package of what would be available at Lord's and commercially orientated negotiations with TCCB would be requested. A small sub-committee was set up to deal with the negotiations. By agreement with Sir Anthony Tuke, counsel's opinion on the TCCB's 'Discussion Paper' was sought, but not shown to the Committee at this time. The opinion was favourable to MCC's current position.

Meanwhile there had been no lack of activity on other fronts. In January of 1983 the Cricket Council, originally formed as the governing body of the game, with equal representation of TCCB, NCA and MCC, had been subjected to changes which left little doubt as to the acquisitive nature of those in power on the TCCB. In one fell swoop, TCCB succeeded in capturing a majority on the Council, instituting a TCCB Chairman and changing the constitution so that all the Council's former powers in connection with the first-class game were delegated irrevocably to the TCCB anyway. The Cricket Council was thus rendered a governing body which had no real power to govern, the MCC representation was reduced to three instead of five. G. O. Allen, a member of the Cricket Council since its inception, had felt bound, at this point, to resign in protest.

As a corollary of this, the TCCB's own powers had become more and more vested in a small executive committee which gradually assumed more responsibilities. Conducting proper arm's-length negotiations was a consummation devoutly to be wished. But would it be possible?

At the same time as the members were approving the working party's final report (May 1984) and MCC's representatives were in the throes of assembling a package to put to TCCB for future peace and harmony on reasonable terms, I first became aware of the significant effect that the rule which prevented the election to the Committee of anyone over seventy, except in exceptional circumstances, might have on the future of the Club. G. O. Allen, now being courted assiduously by members of TCCB, was, because of his great age, not available for re-election. Nor was E. W. Swanton. Gubby Allen was an octogenarian and still an exceptionally powerful figure, Swanton was well into his seventies, and both had done immensely useful work for MCC, Allen over a span of more than forty years. Now neither would be eligible.

Perhaps as a result of the 'seventy rule', which had been insisted upon by the members of the Working Party, it had become more and more apparent that Gubby Allen was shifting his centre from MCC towards TCCB; over the next couple of years this could possibly have been crucial to the outcome.

It was Alex Dibbs, the President in 1984–85 who with the Treasurer, Sir Anthony Tuke, Oliver Popplewell and myself were nominated to negotiate with the TCCB on behalf of MCC, who first made me aware of Gubby's antipathy towards David Clark and me. It was Alex Dibbs who, as he grew more and more into the role of President, and understood at first hand a great many of the problems, who became an ally. It was Alex Dibbs who was a tower of strength in negotiating with TCCB. Ironically, it was Alex Dibbs who made it virtually impossible for the essential outcome to be favourable in a properly negotiated settlement by asking F. G. Mann to be the next President of MCC (at the instigation of Gubby Allen; or so Alex told me later). The custom had always been for the Treasurer and Secretary to be sounded about the appointment of the new President before he was asked. But not this time.

All the TCCB executive had to do was stall for a few months and the possibility of arm's-length negotiations on an MCC-TCCB front would be severely prejudiced. The TCCB set up their own investigations into financial conditions following a proposal from MCC that for every Test match played at Lord's

MCC would guarantee a return to cricket of a sum 100 per cent greater than from any other ground, the match to be played entirely according to TCCB regulations, provided MCC were allowed to run the match on the days in question without interference. MCC's proposals were never properly discussed. Certainly they never came before the TCCB proper. MCC had put forward their formula which appeared to satisfy the reasonable requirements of both sides, only to have it pushed to one side.

At the same time a warning was sounded by Doug Insole, attending an MCC sub-committee meeting, concerning the building of the new Mound stand, that MCC should seek a guarantee from TCCB about the amount of cricket to be played at Lord's in future, before embarking on an expensive project of that nature. Oliver Popplewell, whose guidance had been an inspiration, had become a judge and was much less readily available, otherwise different views might have prevailed. As it was, the threat was regarded with great seriousness and had exactly the desired effect.

So there we were. The ubiquitous George Mann as President designate; Alex Dibbs, his feet firmly under the table, now fully aware of what was going on, and defending MCC's function of running Lord's and increasingly aware of the need to protect the membership. Whether legal opinion, sought with his agreement and that of the Treasurer, which pointed up the dangers of anybody wearing more than one hat during commercial transactions, in which both protagonists were represented by the same person, had had an effect was not easy to gauge. But it is certain he saw the points made by leading counsel through the Club's solicitors. He did not, however, at this stage allow the opinion to go before the Committee, believing, as did David Clark and I, that knowledge of the law was a matter to be used – if at all – as a last resort.

The overall outcome of talks with TCCB during 1985 was stalemate. In spite of the ominously conspicuous absence of any guarantee from TCCB regarding the use of Lord's for major matches, plans for the new stand and the bicentenary went ahead. Symptomatic of the sort of problems faced at that time was the incredible difficulty experienced in trying to get the concept of MCC versus the Rest of the World past the likes of Gubby Allen and George Mann. I was not alone in the occasional thought that there was a move afoot, even within the councils of MCC, to keep the name of MCC out of the title of what was, after all, their own 200th birthday match. Was paranoia creeping in? Possibly, but it was difficult to keep an open mind.

Hard though it was as Secretary of the Club to an incoming President, I knew it was my duty to point out the possible conflicts in the circumstances in which George Mann found himself. President of MCC, recently Chairman of the TCCB and of the Cricket Council, now on the TCCB executive, President of Middlesex: they were appointments of which anyone in the world of cricket would be proud. But all at the same time? Even in a marvellous game like cricket where camaraderie abounds, there were limits to what one Mann could handle. Finally George gave up his seat on the TCCB executive committee.

On the surface, the year passed remarkably well. We were busy with other matters, the World Cup in India and Pakistan and the building of the new Mound stand among them. Negotiations with TCCB appeared to be at a standstill. The 1985 season at Lord's was a success.

The Australians were over and in the year of the Bradford disaster, followed by unfortunate crowd incidents at the end of the Test at Leeds, MCC earned praise from all directions for the public relations and crowd control during the Lord's Test match. I was pleased for the Club and more than a bit pleased for myself when an announcement about crowd behaviour, made on each of the first three days, received applause of astonishing fervour as it echoed round the ground. It helped, too, that other Test match ground secretaries asked for the text.

The performance of the whole MCC Secretariat and staff had been so good that just an inkling of hope remained that TCCB might be persuaded that we could run a Test match.

Another glimmer of encouragement emerged perversely from the findings of the TCCB working party on finances. They had ignored MCC's proposals but had brought forth recommendations damaging to all the Test match grounds. Following levies on members, there were now to be levies on advertising revenue at the Test centres. The deliberations of the working party had taken little or no account of the immense capital costs of running and maintaining a Test match ground entirely at the expense of the incumbent club. So revenue from advertising at the Test match grounds was now TCCB's aim. A series of meetings at Old Trafford called by Cedric Rhoades, the Lancashire Chairman, found the representatives of those grounds united in their opposition to this move.

Resistance to the demands of the TCCB was now being properly organized was for the first time. The Test match grounds asked for an independent assessment by a firm of chartered accountants who had no connection with the interests within cricket. They never got it. The TCCB's own accountants were eventually given the job. At a TCCB meeting held at the end of 1985, the Test match grounds were out-voted by those who stood to benefit largely from the new recommendations. MCC, the great providers, were to be £100,000 worse off in the coming year. Surrey's chief administrator, Raman Subba Row, was the newly elected Chairman of TCCB when the new proposals went through.

The irony was that the new formula preserved the rights of the Test match grounds to their own advertising revenue, but hit hard at previously established incentives aimed at attracting the public to matches. Alone of the Test grounds, MCC had forgone much potential advertising revenue, which would have come to them alone, in favour of allowing several thousand people to sit on the grass. It meant we had trodden a tightrope where crowd control came into the reckoning, but we managed. It also meant that cricket as a whole benefited from the extra money accruing from the larger crowds: all the money from the extra gate came into the pool for distribution to the counties.

Under the new system it paid MCC to replace people with advertising boards, to rely on ancillary income rather than a share of the gate.

It always seemed to me, and many wiser men before me, whatever their affiliations, that any system of financial sharing was best served by giving the Test match grounds as big an incentive as possible to get as many of the cricket-loving public in their grounds as they could. A fixed percentage of the gate and an incentive to take as much money as possible in advance, had seemed an essential part of any package. The new system meant that all such incentives were virtually put on one side. Now, corporate entertainment, the erection of as many advertising signs as possible, and the sale of vast quantities of booze would be the main sources of income. The new wave was upon us.

The Test match grounds had no choice but to accept the TCCB's ruling. Over the years MCC had withstood various assaults on their membership: a gradual erosion of members' privileges and facilities had taken place while MCC had provided more and more money for cricket in general. They had given members' facilities to sponsors; had paid for their members to enter their own ground. They had increased the number of members while failing to increase the facilities available to them.

And so to 1986. J. G. W. Davies had been chosen by George Mann to succeed him as President of MCC. Jack Davies, incumbent in October 1985, had supported his predecessor during the previous summer in his contention that TCCB should be given ultimate authority for major matches played at Lord's. Just what 'ultimate authority' meant in this context had been defined in different ways by different people. But here MCC were embarking on dangerous ground with the Mound stand in progress and fully committed, and the bicentenary just around the corner. In return for their concession the Committee were looking for an undertaking from the TCCB that the pattern of major matches at Lord's would remain unchanged. That undertaking never materialized.

Early in his year of Presidency, Jack Davies, with the agreement of Raman Subba Row, set up a joint TCCB/MCC liaison committee to consider matters relevant to the major matches. It became known as the JLC.

8

THE BEGINNING OF THE END

I HAD VIEWED the first meeting of the JLC, held on 13 December 1985, with some foreboding. There were no clearly defined areas of responsibility agreed before we started. We had apparently abandoned the high ground obtained by MCC putting forward proposals for discussion and implementation on a one-to-one basis and had abandoned proper arm's-length negotiations without getting TCCB to give any sort of satisfactory answer to our proposals. And the process whereby all our promises to the membership, set out in the working party report, were shuffled to one side without the members' knowledge, was now being given an alarming impetus.

On the other hand, talking had to be better than silence. Approach the whole thing, I told myself, in a spirit of sweet reasonableness; the MCC Committee have already given their blessing to your proposals for the 1986 season. No direct damage can be done during the coming summer. It may well be that this won't turn out to be a battle for dominance. Perhaps the TCCB approach will have changed. After all, Subba Row is now the Chairman. All past dealings between us have been amic-able. We have respected each other's points of view, have worked together for a long time now. All those friendly dis-cussions, especially the recent ones, must count for something. Perhaps a real breakthrough will be possible. A fresh start; mutual respect; give and take without compromising essential principles; recognition of MCC's own role at Lord's and recogni-tion that TCCB had a vital overall role in the present and future of cricket.

It became apparent that there was to be no pre-meeting con-ference between MCC's representatives, no discussion of tactics or approach to the agenda. Neither Jack Davies nor Hubert Doggart was available for discussion and no agreed MCC view, as such, was to be put forward on any of the subjects on the agenda. It was, at least on MCC's side, to be a free-for-all. As it turned out, I was cast by Jack Davies, in the chair on this occa-sion, in a leading role.

High on the agenda were arrangements for MCC's bi-centennial match. MCC had already received and obtained the blessing of the member countries of ICC to the participation of players from all over the world. The county clubs had also ex-pressed a firm willingness to help by releasing their players. After a considerable struggle, MCC had been allowed to nego-tiate terms for television coverage of the match. The problem was that TCCB had shown every desire to interfere with arrange-ments, down to the last nut and bolt. So far, the goodwill of cricket in general and some adroit diplomacy had won the day. Now we had to arrive at some formula for financial terms which was acceptable to both sides. MCC had to accept that had it not been for the bicentenary, another Test match could have been scheduled in addition to the five against Pakistan. It concerned me that there had never been a six-match series against Pakistan before, but it had been agreed that some accom-modation should be made so that MCC could not be accused of being niggardly. Accordingly, I had researched the loss of a sixth Test match, based on a sixth Pakistan Test at Lord's and at

Nottingham (where, if there had been one, it would rightfully have been played). The TCCB's 'cabinet' had indicated that the sixth Test would have been at Lord's and so I had to prepare a set of figures, resulting in the much greater sum which would have accrued from a Lord's match.

Based on the information at my disposal, and *assuming additional sponsorship from Cornhill*, the Lord's match would, by my calculations, have realized some £260,000 for cricket. Not until this sum was mentioned and received with approval by Messrs Subba Row, Stevens and Carr, representing TCCB at the JLC meeting, was it mentioned, for the first time by Donald Carr, that the sixth Test would have been not against Pakistan but Sri Lanka. I pointed out that this really was a different cup of tea and was supported by the other MCC representatives in my contention that we should look again at the proposal, this time on the basis of a match against Sri Lanka.

It also had to be argued on MCC's part that a TCCB scheme to stage a series of one-day internationals against the Rest of the World team in addition to compensation for a 'lost' Test match was really a bit much, especially as these would be scheduled almost immediately prior to the bicentenary match itself. A star-studded occasion would be diluted, the effect on the gate was likely to be considerable. Subba Row's long-standing membership of MCC's bicentenary sub-committee helped save the day and it was agreed that this would be too much of a good thing, not least because of the effect of even more international cricket on the county championship and other domestic competitions. Besides, MCC *were* paying all the costs associated with the Rest of the World team.

This first Joint Liaison Committee looked also at the TCCB Chairman's conviction that credit cards should be accepted at Lord's. They were not to be in 1986. Not only had all seats been sold without them but MCC would have had to employ more staff to administer the procedure, and – another telling point – why should cricket be deprived of 2.6 per cent of Lord's income when no more would come through the gate as a result?

We would, however, look at it in a true spirit of co-operation and make recommendations to the MCC Committee for 1987. Another matter of moment was whether MCC were right to limit the number of tickets obtainable by any one applicant, to ensure a fair distribution to as many people as possible and for reasons of security.

Having been given the task of making most of the running at the meeting itself, I was also charged with writing the minutes and agreeing them with my opposite number on the TCCB, Donald Carr. It had been a sensible meeting, I thought, and Hubert Doggart with whom I talked afterwards was enthusiastic. We both agreed that Subba Row had shown a welcome sense of proportion and that auguries for the future were promising. Certainly there was nothing in my mind which prepared me for what lay round the corner.

I had deliberately delayed writing the draft minutes until the results of the meeting had been relayed to the MCC Committee by the President, J. G. W. Davies. I delayed primarily because, having played a prominent part in the JLC meeting, I wanted to check that the President's report coincided with my own notes and memory of what had taken place. The pressure of normal work for both MCC and ICC was also immense. It was with a light heart that I sat down to draft the minutes over the Christmas holiday. The President's report to the Committee had confirmed the essence of the meeting and was in complete harmony with my own recollections. After several days my minutes were returned by Donald Carr, with his Chairman's approval. There were no suggestions correcting a nuance here, an emphasis there; the odd hint that such-and-such, if rephrased, would suit better. Instead, words were crossed out for no apparent reason and others substituted with no obvious improvement. It was in tone the direct antithesis of everything Doggart and I had discussed so sanguinely. None of it made sense to me in the context of a new beginning.

I consulted Jack Davies at the earliest opportunity which happened to be after the memorial service for Alex Dibbs, who had succumbed to a stroke some months previously. I pointed out the problem with which we were faced. He agreed that the minutes, as returned to me, did not tally with his own recollections. As the alterations had been sanctioned, according to Donald Carr, by the Chairman of the TCCB, I asked Davies to take up the matter with his opposite number. He declined, saying that it was up to me to sort it out: the terms of reference for the Joint Liaison Committee had stated that the minutes should be agreed by the Secretaries of the respective bodies. So I took a deep swallow, and spent some hours preparing a new set of minutes, incorporating many of the phrases used by TCCB in their corrected draft, but keeping the main thrust and the decisions as I had originally drafted, and as already reported by the President to the MCC Committee.

I submitted this set of minutes to the Secretary of TCCB. Unwisely, as it turned out, I also sent a covering letter indicating that if these minutes were not acceptable, the next JLC meeting, due in five days' time, would have to decide what *was* a true record of the meeting. It was a particularly hectic week and my covering letter, though not rude, could have been phrased more diplomatically. But I did feel aggrieved that what had seemed a promising meeting should result in needless problems over the minutes.

What happened next was the beginning of the end.

The second meeting of the Joint Liaison Committee took place on 24 January. It was preceded by a conversational lunch in the MCC Committee dining-room. It was Subba Row's turn to take the chair, MCC having been responsible for chairing the first meeting. He led off with a harangue of startling ferocity, blaming me for my behaviour over the minutes and deploring the way 'the Board' (the TCCB) had been treated. If its purpose was to disadvantage the MCC representation, it certainly succeeded. Hardly a word was said in reply; and I was clearly in no position to say anything in self-justification, believing that now was not the time to enter any sort of fray. Besides, such was the venom of the attack that I was virtually in a state of shock. Worse was to come.

Following some apologetic noises from the MCC side of the table, it was agreed that the third set of minutes should be regarded as a true record of the previous meeting. Arising from these minutes there was the question of compensation to TCCB, by MCC, for the loss of the sixth Test match. Since the last meeting, I had, with the help of John Lawrence, MCC's accountant, prepared figures in relation to a Test played by England against Sri Lanka at Lord's. Only one Test match had ever been played against Sri Lanka in England and that had been at Lord's in August 1984. It had been a comparatively easy task to project the figures for that match forward to 1987, taking into account inflation, increased television fees and so on. During our researches we had, however, discovered one important factor, information which had only recently come to our attention. It concerned the contract drawn up with Cornhill on behalf of all members of TCCB including MCC. And it made a considerable difference to our calculations.

At the first Joint Liaison Committee I had put forward suggestions which I believed to be realistic and which had been treated as such by the TCCB trio. Included in these had been a large sum to account for the sponsorship fee I had assumed would have been paid to TCCB in the event of a sixth Test match. I had since discovered that a total sum would be payable to TCCB in 1987 however many Tests were scheduled. In other words, the notion of any additional sponsorship money could be ruled right out of our calculations and was something we should not have been taking into account when putting forward a sum for compensation, based on a Pakistan match, at that first meeting; although doing so had brought no argument from the TCCB representatives.

I duly went through each stage of my reasoning. The atmosphere, made less than congenial by Raman's outburst, developed a distinctly icy touch when I explained that for the purpose of this exercise it would be wrong to include any sponsorship fee. When it was further pointed out that comparison based on a sixth Test at Lord's against Sri Lanka now came to much less than half the £260,000 previously put forward, a polar bear would have felt chilly. I hastened to point out that MCC would presumably expect to pay compensation to counties for the release of their players in addition to an overall sum, and searched around frantically for anything else which might soften the blow. But by now there was little hope of damage limitation. I was told later that Subba Row had reported earlier to his executive that TCCB could be receiving approximately £260,000 from MCC.

I pointed out that nothing but tentative talks had been held at the first meeting and all that had happened here was that we had put forward figures based on a formula which we hoped would be verifiable and acceptable. No deal had to be struck on these lines, although it seemed the fairest way to arrive at a suitable figure.

The meeting then continued without further incident and a date was arranged for the next meeting. Donald Carr would be writing the minutes.

That evening, the Test and County Cricket Board were giving a dinner at Lord's for the England party who would be setting out the following day to tour the West Indies. The MCC Committee dining-room was used for the occasion. Raman Subba Row was in the chair. A number of the gods of cricket, past and present, sat down to dine. Jack Davies and I were guests; though in a sense, as President and Secretary of MCC, we were representing those whose facilities were being used. It was as much fun as it could be, in all the circumstances. Ian Botham and Allan Lamb sat opposite me, Peter May on my right. Peter made a few remarks to me about the afternoon's meeting. I responded. It was all very civilized. I exchanged my larger helping of meat for Ian Botham's smaller one and it was gratefully received. Raman Subba Row made a speech in which he counselled the team that a smile would work wonders in the West Indies. It was to prove a tour which saw English smiles at something of a premium, but at that time, though many of us expected the worst, optimism was not out of place.

As it turned out, any optimistic thoughts I had nurtured during the evening that the afternoon's proceedings hadn't been so bad after all, were to receive a severe jolt. Most of the party had disappeared when I approached Raman, asked if I could get him a drink, got him one and then had my ears pinned back.

'I don't understand you,' he said. 'Who the hell do you think you are?'

I was baffled, nonplussed.

'I'm sorry we seem to have got off to such a bad start with the Joint Liaison Committee,' I said. 'I'm sorry if you think it's my fault. It is my job to look after the interests of MCC and that's all I think I've been doing. Certainly I haven't wanted to offend you or anyone else. I must admit to being surprised when you had such a go at me this afternoon.'

'Do you realize you are paid twice as much as me?' was his next remark. 'You travel all over the world. You are involved with every aspect of the game. What is it you want?'

While turning over in my mind these seemingly unconnected observations, I answered that as Secretary of MCC I felt I should be in a position to run Lord's at the behest of the MCC Committee. That was really all I wanted to be able to do. I wanted to co-operate in every possible way with the TCCB, short of handing over Lord's or selling MCC and its members short. I enjoyed my work on behalf of ICC and looked forward to being in Jamaica in a couple of months' time.

'I've talked to Jack Davies,' he went on. 'I shall be writing to him. You and I must meet before I do. But if you don't want to join our party, you will have to go.' End of conversation.

It was reported to me later, I think by Jack Davies, that Raman had been goaded by members of his executive committee over the question of the new figure of compensation to TCCB, he having reported the outcome of the afternoon's meeting. The thought that he had been outwitted, or set-up may have been put into his mind. Certainly, the reception he appeared to have received had not made him kindly disposed towards me.

Looking back I could not have played it much differently, but I was concerned that a chance of peace with honour to both sides looked likely to go down the river. Concerned, too, that it could be made to look as though it was my fault that it had happened.

The following morning I wrote a letter of apology to Raman Subba Row and a similar letter to Donald Carr. I wrote, not because I felt guilty or necessarily wrong, but because I was prepared to do almost anything at that stage to prevent a breach which could not be healed. I genuinely did not want to fall out with Raman, a friend of many years' standing, nor did I want MCC's position in delicate negotiations to be compromised by what could only be a misunderstanding. It may well have been a mistake and seen as a sign of weakness on my part. Certainly it did nothing to ease the situation outwardly; quite the reverse.

Following the receipt of my letter and before Raman and I could meet to discuss things over a drink, as we had agreed to do, Jack Davies was sent a letter, uncompromising in tone, unequivocal in its message. Subba Row was on a trail I knew of old, one which I had seen trodden with sponsors and others: the hard-line approach, a march through all the courtesies and niceties, a refusal to budge until he either got his way or his bluff was called by experts in the same field. I had known him forced to climb down once, by the managing director of Gillette during negotiations for the sponsorship of the Gillette Cup, but then a pretty robust approach had been adopted by Gillette. Would the MCC Committee be prepared to fight fire with fire? Their record was, on the whole, one of taking the middle road. Clearly compromise would be necessary, but how far could the Committee (or at least those members of it who were not already at the nub of a bid for power at Lord's) be persuaded that the cause of the Club and its members was of paramount importance? The outlook appeared to be wet and windy with sudden squalls. But clearly, the Club were up against a most difficult and searching problem.

The letter from Raman Subba Row caused great consternation and concern all round, and pinned all the blame fairly and squarely on my shoulders for what was indicated to be frustration of his best intentions and an absence on my part of any real desire to co-operate with 'the Board'. He also intimated that I had clearly registered a message that the joint liaison initiatives should be wound up at the earliest opportunity.

He went on to say that the TCCB were not prepared to carry on meeting MCC until such time as MCC resolved the problem. It was up to them how they did it.

I sent all the papers, letters and reports concerning the Joint Liaison Committee and its break-up to the MCC Committee. A meeting of the full Committee was held to consider these papers, and the position at large, on 9 April 1986.

Not all the MCC Committee, in considering this latest turn of events, were aware that they were doing so against a background of such long-standing controversy. The nuances of the issue between MCC and TCCB, which was essentially whether MCC should be allowed to run Lord's, or whether at certain times of their own choosing, with or without warning, TCCB should take over control, was perhaps imperfectly understood by the newer members. Although it was never stated as such, what those in the centre of power on the TCCB seemed to want was a right of action without reference to MCC; or, if reference were made, an acceptance by MCC that whatever TCCB wanted at Lord's they would get. As members of TCCB, the Club acknowledged an obligation, even a duty, to go along willingly with decisions affecting the organization of programmes within the Test and county arena, whatever the inconvenience to the Club. The role of TCCB as co-ordinators of the first-class game was never in doubt. This parting of the ways, no wider at first than a hair-line crack, but developing over the years into a schism, had its origins in a flexing of muscles, a thrust for power by the TCCB centre, within the confines of Lord's; and a reluctance by MCC to grant *carte blanche* in their own house to an organization which suddenly sought power without responsibility – responsibility vested in the MCC Committee by its members. MCC owned the place and were proud and jealous of its traditions and its reputation.

MCC, then, readily acknowledged TCCB's overall responsibility for the staging of a series of matches and for decisions related to that purlieu. That was the responsibility handed down by the Cricket Council, the game's governing body, where TCCB and MCC originally shared equal status with the National Cricket Association.

MCC wanted to control the resources at their disposal, to be in sole direction of their staff, and they wanted to run their own ground and the cricket at the time it was being played. They were happy to continue to give TCCB, the NCA and Middlesex accommodation; very happy to work hard for cricket internationally through the International Cricket Conference, although only the President and Secretary were involved in this sphere of activity; pleased and honoured to be entrusted with responsibility for the Laws of the game.

Dual management of Lord's, or haphazardly scheduled involvement in the running of the place, was bound to be questioned. However friendly, gifted or respected those seeking control might be, it was the MCC Committee, with the Secretariat and staff at the sharp end, who had responsibility for the well being and integrity of Lord's. A philosophy of help and guidance, rather than cajolement, had been at the heart of the MCC's own reign. For the six or so years of its existence up to 1974, the TCCB had trodden much the same path. But then, both bodies had been administered professionally by the same people. Now things were different.

It was a sensitive time. Donald Carr and I shared more than one bottle of whisky trying to agree every detail of our varied responsibilities. Would that we had been of one mind. The general aim was similar. We had worked together harmoniously for both MCC and TCCB, but now there were (inevitably I suppose) differences of opinion about the respective roles of MCC and TCCB at Lord's.

My own views were born of soundings taken within the MCC Committee. Future policy was laid down by them and, in detail, at several meetings of chairmen of MCC sub-committees, called specifically for the purpose, with G. O. Allen as he then was, in the chair.

Throughout this introductory period to the pressures that lay ahead, G. O. Allen was the Treasurer of MCC. He had been around so long, had sat on so many committees, was so quick and agile of mind and had a foot in so many different camps, that he was the nearest thing cricket had to an *éminence grise*. Since there was no real king at the time, Gubby Allen was as powerful as it was possible to be. His was the ear above all others to bend if you wanted your views to be accepted. His was the voice to which every ear was open. He was certainly at my side during those early years as Secretary of the Club. He it was who laid down the overall pattern to be followed in helping MCC to keep its footing and, give or take a few hairy moments, we found ourselves in agreement about most things concerning the Club. 'With your intelligence and my experience,' he once said to me, 'MCC will achieve its rightful place in the game.'

He was clear that MCC's sovereignty at Lord's should be respected and maintained, while he was Treasurer of the Club, just as I was throughout my Secretaryship. He had a winning way and much charm and he was absolutely unerring and instinctively clever when it came to keeping himself in the centre of what was going on. This was to be an important factor, even after he left office, and long after he relinquished any official position of power.

The relationship between those at the centre of TCCB and MCC had survived a number of small but serious disturbances, some of which had their origins in the appointment of Peter Lush as public relations and promotions officer to the Cricket Council and the TCCB. Lush had arrived on the scene after Raman Subba Row, who had first been offered the job (which I had recently vacated), had decided that the conditions imposed on the occupant were not to his liking and had refused it. Lord

Caccia, Billy Griffith, Donald Carr and I among others had been deputed to deal with the appointment, and we felt that the job should carry with it day-to-day responsibility to the Secretary of the Cricket Council and the TCCB, Donald Carr. Raman was not prepared to be responsible to any specific person. There must also have been doubt in his mind as to whether he would have to sever connections with his own public relations company in the City while serving cricket in a professional capacity.

To loosen the reins to the extent that Raman apparently wanted posed a threat to the whole amateur/professional administrative structure of the time.

Peter Lush came to us from an advertising agency and apparently accepted the guidelines laid down for the job. It soon became fairly clear, however, that the old style of working would not apply. Certainly as someone supposed to be responsible to the MCC Committee for Lord's cricket ground, I was faced with a number of difficult situations. These were embarrassing because commitments had been made, without MCC's knowledge, which affected Lord's, the membership and sometimes the whole ambience of the place. I had, for instance, to disabuse the marketing manager of Gillette Industries of the notion that we could entertain the free distribution of razor products to the crowd at the Gillette Cup final, although he had been told by a TCCB representative that this was perfectly in order. Crowd behaviour was a constant problem even in the far off days of the mid-1970s, and here was a hazard at which the MCC Committee looked askance.

MCC were keen to help sponsorship of the game overall by extending generous facilities to sponsors at Lord's, but they were none too keen to find deals being virtually sealed without proper consultation beforehand. Nor were matters helped when in order to increase sponsorship fees, which impressed the counties, sources of income, such as advertising signs, free seats which could easily be sold, and boxes were being thrown into packages for sponsors and were draining MCC's own income as a result. MCC were far from niggardly but if their resources were to be re-allocated, they wanted more say in how it was to be done.

Peter Lush's independent outlook also produced sources of irritation during the staging of matches at Lord's. More happens, minute by minute, behind the scenes, than the average spectator dreams of. Even on the quietest of days the best laid plans can go astray and it was a matter of pride that MCC should keep their fingers on the pulse throughout, having done all the administration from the time the first ticket was sold. It was therefore no help to have reports filtering through that BBC radio had just announced that there was still plenty of room on the ground when we knew that all the tickets had been sold.

More serious, perhaps, were occasions when pressure was put on me to do things at short notice which I felt were intrinsically wrong. One of several examples will serve to illustrate the point.

The Benson and Hedges Cup final was washed out on the Saturday. Lord's has been exceptionally lucky with its Cup final weather as a rule, but this day was a snorter and it was soon obvious that play would be necessary on the next day set aside – the following Monday. The match was a sell-out. Tickets had been distributed for every seat. On the back of each ticket as always was printed words to the effect that it would be available for entry into the ground or to the seat in question on any day the match was played. During that rain-sodden Saturday I was approached with the proposition that on Monday we should allow people into the ground without a ticket and on payment, and that a statement to this effect should be made. The theory was that not many ticket holders would turn up and more money could be made as a result. I was up against some fast bowling on a sticky wicket: MCC's (not TCCB's) reputation was at stake. It was quite possible that an unquantifiable number of ticket holders would not turn up on Monday. On the other hand, might they not give their ticket to someone who could? In any case, we could not know the answer until late on

Monday afternoon. Ticket holders might well decide to make an appearance after work. An over-riding, if old-fashioned, consideration was the awful feeling that selling seats twice was not a good thing to be doing.

Although under considerable pressure, I refused. Fortunately for me the ground was nearly full when the last ball was bowled on the Monday. But should I really have been put in that position at all? Nor did my being right on that and several other difficult occasions help matters: quite the reverse. The fact that every decision had been the result of consultation with the MCC Secretariat and staff who were fully behind me, and on occasion well ahead, was some consolation. But it made no difference to the real issue, which was a strong desire by TCCB's inner circle to have entirely selective power and authority at Lord's – this despite the facts that they were short on background knowledge and that MCC were doing a reasonable job. As much as anything they wanted to be *thought* to be in charge.

It was difficult to see a sensible ending to it all. Nobody really wanted to see the TCCB leave Lord's. But on a day-to-day, week-to-week basis, it was possible to see some advantage in their being on the same footing as other associations which had an overall responsibility for co-ordinating the affairs of its members such as the Football Association, the Lawn Tennis Association, the Confederation of British Industry and so on. Of course cricket was not the same thing and on the whole it would have been an ungracious gesture on MCC's part not to build new offices for the TCCB, the Cricket Council, the NCA and Middlesex, as they did at considerable cost to the membership.

A favourite dictum of the TCCB executive was that what was good for one Test match ground was good for them all: all were the same. This was promulgated whatever the subject matter. It was a dogma which ignored the fact that Lord's and all the other Test grounds were different from each other in many material ways. It was a useful way of roping in administrators to do things against their better judgement. Ring up X and tell him you want something done. Tell him the other grounds have agreed to it. Most people will accept for fear of going against the majority. Add to this the fact that the Test match grounds were outvoted on the TCCB by thirteen votes to six and what was going from the Test grounds was coming to the others, and the grounds were occasionally put into an embarrassing position. None of this would have mattered very much had not some of the issues involved cut right into the heart of the traditional values and, at times, the finances of a Test match club.

Packer had come and gone; after a faltering start the TCCB and MCC, through their stewardship of the International Cricket Conference, had co-operated well in the face of what was then seen as the common enemy. We had lost the battle hands down, but there was room to believe that the experience could be good for the game not only in the UK, but throughout the world.

It was a pity, therefore, that the TCCB should introduce, almost before the dust was settled, a levy on Test match grounds based on the number of members from that particular club who attended Test matches. The move posed problems for all the Test grounds. But none was harder hit than MCC. It was not so much a question of the finance involved, which could have been provided in any number of ways; it was a blow in the vitals to the very principle of membership of MCC. Stands at Lord's are provided for members and their friends. Other parts of the ground are for paying customers. Many members choose to pay for what they consider to be better seats, but that is up to them. Forcing the members to pay for admission to their own ground, built out of Club funds, maintained by Club funds with no help from elsewhere, at a time when MCC were providing immensely more to TCCB than they received from central funds (unlike any other club in the country), was a shock to the system. To begin with, Donald Carr and others insisted that all Test match grounds should collect money from members at the gate. The MCC Committee persuaded themselves that in spite of the principle involved, they would pay the Danegeld, but the money due from MCC members who actually came to a Test match at Lord's and were meticulously counted, would be provided pro rata from the club funds. Thus the levy, though briefly mentioned in the Annual Report, was largely hidden from the membership. For the sake of peace and quiet it was just as well.

The next levy on members really caused a rumpus, but this should be seen in the context of a number of other events which had happened along the way.

In a general sense, it was the view of the MCC Committee, or at least the majority, who were not locked into the TCCB inner circle – and this applied even though four or five individuals were replaced every year – that Lord's should reflect MCC. Continuous buffeting on the subject of how far TCCB should share in the organization of the place by, for instance, taking over the issuing of passes to the ground, taking over responsibility for the entertainment of guests from home and overseas, taking over responsibility for crowd control and presentation procedures, making decisions of policy during matches – the list was endless – had been, in the main, turned to one side. It had taken its toll, however, and for a time the Committee had agreed to the blurring of the edges of certain hitherto clear-cut realms of responsibility. The unhappy consequences had been seen most publicly during the Centenary Test match against Australia in 1980, played at Lord's, and giving rise to much controversy. Among several other disturbing features was a loss of play, for no good discernible reason, on the Saturday and the jostling of the umpires by certain MCC members. Without going into details of the whole unfortunate business, the general message was there to be seen quite plainly. If MCC were to take the blame – which they did – then they must retain control over their own operation.

To help keep the peace TCCB were given two boxes at Lord's instead of one, and entertainment facilities were enlarged at the expense of MCC's members. This did little to allay the stream of requests for additional concessions. In his day as my assistant secretary on the cricket side, John Lofting referred to these tactics pursued through the years as blanket-bombing. It certainly felt like that at times.

9

A WAY THROUGH THE WOOD

FOLLOWING THE LAST meeting of the Joint Liaison Committee, Subba Row's letter to the President and the circulation of all correspondence in that connection to members of the MCC Committee, it was time to take stock for the umpteenth time and from as many angles as possible. The scorecard had an interesting look about it, but the home team's potential and will to win had to be doubted.

This left those who wished to preserve what they felt to be the integrity and traditional values of MCC and Lord's. They were the nucleus of a strong team but they would all have to play well if a satisfactory result was to be obtained. There was my good friend the Treasurer, David Clark. There was more than half of the Committee. There was the President, J. G. W. Davies, committed to find a solution based on TCCB's ultimate authority (whatever that meant) but finding that intellectual solutions are often less effective in practice than in theory, because people are involved at every stage. There could be no question that his heart was in the right place. There were my colleagues on the MCC Secretariat. They had experienced the day-to-day problems, the continuous war of attrition; I had kept them fully informed at every turn and had found them in complete agreement (unsurprisingly) when it came to sustaining MCC's position at Lord's while co-operating to the fullest possible extent with TCCB. There was the Club's solicitor, backed by opinions from more than one leading counsel, who from reading of the Club's rules, the Committee's endorsement of the working party report, and their knowledge of the TCCB Constitution, had suggested MCC made clear to TCCB that:

> Except specifically by contract with MCC, TCCB has no right or power to take away or in any way diminish the powers of the MCC Committee in connection with Lord's cricket ground or MCC's property; to dictate what should or should not be the rights of members at Lord's; or to direct MCC's employees in any way as to the manner in which such employees carry out their duties.
>
> Any principle TCCB sought to establish should be compatible with the above.

That was one piece of advice on MCC's position, as members of TCCB, following the production of TCCB's 'Discussion Report' in 1983.

There was eminent counsel's view, with which successive Presidents had been acquainted, written in July 1984, making it clear that those with one or more hats, and sitting on the MCC Committee and (say) the TCCB Executive, should be wary of getting involved in decisions which affected MCC commercially or materially. Civil action could result.

Consideration of the correspondence between Raman Subba Row and Jack Davies, which had led to the breakdown of the Joint Liaison Committee, took place at the beginning of April 1986. The Committee as a whole could not accept that Subba Row's letter had been justified. Nor could they accept that his attitude was warranted. They saw that he was going straight for my jugular, but they felt it best to continue trying to find a way back to sanity. Talks had already taken place between Subba Row and Jack Davies in Jamaica, but no satisfactory outcome was in evidence. The Committee asked the President to make an approach in the spirit of compromise, but to make it clear that the Secretary had received the support of the Committee and would not be excluded from discussions. The TCCB should indicate, taking the last Test match at Lord's as an example, what they would like to have seen done differently. A list of suggested improvements was called for.

It was not forthcoming.

Instead, a sustained and single-minded attack on the Secretary of MCC was mounted by Subba Row with the apparent approval of his Executive Committee. He wrote to the Chairmen of all county clubs about me and my 'attitude'. He attacked me and my colleagues in the Secretariat in further correspondence. Differences between MCC and TCCB of a genuine nature were now being personalized.

Individual members of the MCC Committee, especially those who were playing major parts in the organization of the MCC bicentenary, or the building of the new Mound stand, were regaled with tales of the Secretary's iniquities and his failure to brief the MCC Committee in the past. This was utterly, and justly, refuted by David Clark, the MCC Treasurer, in a letter to Subba Row, and he was supported in this by those on the Committee who knew the facts of the matter over a number of years.

David Clark received scant thanks from some members of the MCC Committee for his intervention. It seemed that in their eyes he was further complicating an issue which they had hoped was becoming less complicated.

Gradually, during the summer of 1986, the screw was tightened. Bit by bit, cracks, already apparent in the foundation stone of the MCC Committee's thinking throughout the year, were widening. A few were in favour of getting rid of the problem on any terms the TCCB put forward. It would be damned inconvenient if the matter became public. The ship was still afloat, but had slowed perceptibly. Then Subba Row spelled out, in a letter to MCC's President, that TCCB were not merely seeking ultimate authority for the staging of matches at Lord's with the minimum of interference and the maximum of delegation (the 1983 document), but also overall authority and control, as well as the right of ongoing supervision and monitoring of arrangements at Lord's cricket ground. It was clear that the TCCB were moving fast into the realms of complete domination.

This did something to stiffen the sinews of waverers, but the twin threats to Test matches and the bicentenary were strong medicine. The TCCB were asked if they would accept arbitration by a mutually agreed and respected neutral figure. On behalf of the TCCB, Subba Row said no. MCC asked if TCCB would accept an undertaking from MCC which gave TCCB ultimate authority, but with caveats in respect of the rights of MCC members and the Secretariat and staff of MCC. Again the answer was unhelpful. Subba Row wrote that TCCB would accept no caveats!

Uppermost in the minds of several of us, while all this was going on, was the threat to MCC's membership if complete control was surrendered to the TCCB in the way they wanted. There was a threat to the membership, but the Committee's integrity *vis-à-vis* the membership was also at stake. The working party report stated clearly the Committee's aims and intentions. The membership had adopted the document, thereby getting the Committee off the hook. Was it not right that before employing another tack, let alone a *completely* different one, the membership should be consulted? If the membership agreed that matches at Lord's should be taken over in the way TCCB wanted, having had the matter properly explained, my own convictions and those of many of us would have to go by the board. The members would have spoken.

It was time to see the Club's solicitor again. In June 1986 a joint opinion by two leading counsel was received. It was clear in their view that MCC through the Committee should seek clarification of the extent and meaning of any commitment asked for by TCCB. They should negotiate the best possible deal and present the resultant package to the members for direction.

Counsel took this view, not just because it was a procedure which appeared to follow from the working party report, but for two other reasons. First, as members of a private club, the members should not have their rights affected without their consent, unless there had been some specific delegation by them to the Committee. Second, counsel expressed further concern about the potential conflict of interest relating to those members of the MCC Committee who had a foot in both camps.

It seemed clear to me that the Committee ought to consult the members before making any final commitment along the lines requested by TCCB. Most laymen feel it is sensible to follow legal advice, but apart from this the TCCB ought to know that the membership would be involved if the TCCB persisted in what seemed impossible demands from a sensible management point of view where Lord's was concerned. And they ought really to know just how far their rights were in jeopardy. And it was right that they should make a decision based on all the information at the Committee's disposal. This would take time, but it would show the TCCB that we were in earnest, and they could hardly take matches away from us because we were consulting our members.

At the MCC Committee meeting in July 1986, I, at the President's request, mentioned that legal opinion had been sought, and offered to circulate copies. References to the conflicts of interest between MCC and TCCB were no surprise to the President as, like successive Presidents before him, he had been made fully aware of the issues involved. Indeed, on occasion, Doug Insole on the TCCB Executive had been asked not to attend an MCC Committee meeting to avoid the inherent problems. Not that this mattered greatly, since as much talk about the subject was taking place outside the Committee as in it, but at least some semblance of form was preserved in this one case. But there was a body of opinion among the Committee which would not countenance the circulation of counsels' opinion. At the President's insistence I read out the joint counsels' opinion which advised going to the membership, and told those present that copies were available. Not everybody present availed themselves of the opportunity of reading this opinion, but at least they had all heard it.

When asked what I thought should happen next, I indicated that at the very least it seemed inevitable that the TCCB should be informed that unless they accepted both caveats put forward in the last letter, the Committee would go to the membership. This advice was not accepted, although supported by a number of others. Thus, I believe, went MCC's one real chance of solving the matter with honour.

During this meeting it became clear that a number of those present, F. G. Mann among them, thought the Secretary of MCC should take orders from the Secretary of TCCB about how affairs at Lord's were conducted. The Secretary of MCC would have no right of refusal and would be expected to convey instructions to his staff without question. What happened was that the MCC President wrote a letter to the Chairman of TCCB. The TCCB's overall and ultimate responsibility for staging matches at Lord's was recognized. The full co-operation of the MCC Secretariat with TCCB was also stated in clear terms as having been given. With all that had gone before, and remained on the record, it was complete capitulation.

The President asked in return for an assurance that the traditional programme at Lord's would continue. He also indicated that MCC had inescapable legal obligations in respect of MCC members, so that if TCCB exercised their responsibilities in a way that seriously affected members' rights, MCC would be bound to consult members before action was taken.

No written reply was forthcoming from the TCCB.

The next meeting, between three members of MCC and some members of the TCCB, was held in my absence. Throughout the 1986 negotiations MCC had been firmly of the opinion that any formal meetings with TCCB should be held in my presence. It became obvious that certain members of the Committee could not understand why this should be, but it was clear to the majority that anything else was an unacceptable condition of resuming talks on an official basis. Unacceptable or not, such a meeting *was* held. When the meeting took place on a day when I was away from Lord's MCC were represented by the President, Jack Davies; the treasurer, David Clark; Sir Anthony Tuke; and Colin Cowdrey. Raman Subba Row was in the chair.

The TCCB representatives produced a list of items which were of concern to them, and evidence of MCC's shortcomings, probably drawn up by Peter Lush and Donald Carr. The effect on most members of the Committee (and, later, on me) was one of amazement that so much fuss had been made about items of such a nature. The points raised now and in previous correspondence included: a requirement for the Chairman of TCCB to accompany the President of MCC and the Queen onto the pitch when Her Majesty visited Lord's (a point never previously mentioned); the fact that all the MCC Committee should be present in the MCC Committee Room when the Queen arrived, together with TCCB representatives, which was considered to be all too many. (Presumably MCC would have to shed some of their people.) There was a notion that MCC's organization of the match in question should cease while presentations to the teams were made and that TCCB should take over this part of the action, thus taking over from MCC's President and Secretary; that TCCB should be included in announcements made to the public welcoming them to Lord's; that accommodation reserved for members of MCC and their friends should be available for any guests TCCB chose to invite, over and above the two hundred or so seats already set aside for hospitality; a request for more of the MCC members' boxes. (The membership were already deprived of up to 30 per cent of these.) And so it went on. Most items were capable of resolution by the MCC Committee. It was up to them. Giving up their *right* to decide was the real sticking point. One item did set the majority by the ears. It called into question whether MCC should have a bicentenary match at all, and if so whether they or TCCB should produce programmes for it.

By now we had reached August 1986. Conversations I had held with various Committee members, most of whom were genuinely concerned for my position and welfare, notably Michael Sissons who did his level best to make me see how matters lay, led me to the conclusion that to a number of the MCC Committee, total acceptance of the TCCB demands was preferable to either resistance on grounds of principle or the need for a sensible structure of management. It also seemed certain that a number of the Committee were prepared to wash their hands of the whole matter provided it went away and they did not have to enter into further soul-searching and wearing discussion of what was becoming tedious. There were of course members of the MCC Committee firmly wedded to TCCB ideals, and the incoming President, Colin Cowdrey, was continually making noises as though he was one of them.

How far could I go, bearing in mind my responsibility to the members, and my own set of bourgeois principles, and bearing in mind that, to the TCCB, co-operation, which had always been forthcoming in many ways from MCC, meant submission? The answer was, 'Not very much further!'

But it seemed upon reflection that it would be unreasonable to expect the Secretary of MCC to pursue, in the course of his duties, activities which were either illegal or quasi-legal. I wrote a paper to that effect for perusal by the MCC Committee. It read as follows:

> I feel it only right, in view of assurances having been given to TCCB regarding the full co-operation of the Secretariat, to clarify and seek the Committee's understanding of my own position and indeed the position that any Secretary of MCC would find himself in, under present conditions.
>
> While wishing to co-operate fully with TCCB on many

matters, I fear that there are certain areas where either lawfully, quasi-lawfully or in the interests of the Club and its members, the Secretary would be bound to question and indeed fail to implement certain possible requirements.

Although there may never be the need to do so, the Secretary may find himself, as indeed I have been in the past, having to refuse a suggestion, as it then was, or an order, as it may become, which is not only against the best interests of the Club but questionable legally.

In this instance I cite the pressure put on me to sell seats at Lord's twice over at a Benson and Hedges final and the pressure put on the Club to change at impossibly short notice the days of play in the Centenary Test match, which would have meant that Monday became the fifth day of the match – many tickets for the match having been sold on the basis that it was the fourth day, which has always been a much more popular day than the fifth.

Despite opinions expressed to the contrary at a recent Committee meeting, the Secretary of MCC simply could not accept such an order.

Other areas of concern include the following:

The position of the Secretary of MCC is that he has statutory duties under the Safety of Sports Grounds Act. These duties include the proper carrying out of all matters relating to crowd control and the safety of a crowd at Lord's.

Related to these aspects would need to be careful consideration of all matters relating to the housing of a large crowd, including the following:

(a) sales of tickets to the public
(b) accommodation of the public
(c) all security aspects including direct responsibility of MCC for admission to the ground at all times.

By the very nature of his duties, the Secretary would also

be responsible, whether he liked it or not, for having to decline to comply with requests or orders which could affect the members' rights in any way as to privileges or finance except under direct orders from the Committee of MCC unless the ICC Committee had wholly handed over responsibility for seeing that these rights were safeguarded or otherwise, to another body, presumably with the prior permission of the members.

Finally, the Secretary who was worth his salt could not accept directions which made life either impossible or exceptionally onerous for those employed by MCC to carry out duties within the context of the decision involved. It would not be possible to say 'yes' under such circumstances.

A special meeting of the MCC Committee was called for September 1986. In front of them the Committee had my paper, having had ample time to read it. The President reported, bringing the content of his latest discussion with Subba Row before the Committee. Prior to the meeting, I had suggested to the President that the Committee had several courses of action open to them. Clearly one course was to get rid of the Secretary. I believed that dismissal would be quite contrary to the provisions of the Act regarding legal and wrongful dismissal. I thought that the time had come for the Committee to take stock. Either they could go to the members with the full facts of the MCC/TCCB contretemps or they could come to terms with TCCB demands. If they did the latter, clearly this put me in a vulnerable position in view of the paper I had written, which was at odds with some of those demands.

It was of course open to MCC to call the TCCB's bluff and agree to stage matches under the same conditions as they had always done, but seeking to co-operate with TCCB in every way short of conceding rights of control and interference. It was stretching the imagination to suppose that the Committee would take this course, or they would have done so much earlier.

Discussion on the subject took place in the absence of myself and my colleagues on the Secretariat. We were absent for an hour and a half. Upon my re-entering the Committee Room, the President informed me that the Committee had unanimously agreed that for the Secretary to leave office was not in any way an alternative to be considered. The President would prepare guidelines for future reference which would marry with the 'bottom line' paper I had written.

10

A TIME FOR REFLECTION

Now it was time for everyone to draw breath. The end
of the 1986 cricket season, marked at Lord's by the Nat-
West Trophy final, was as good a time as any. The President
wrote to Subba Row. He explained that MCC were disappointed that all the assurances given in good faith should have
been met with scepticism. MCC's undertaking to co-operate
should, he said, be given a fair trial. This meant TCCB and
MCC getting together on matters of common interest. Guidelines were being prepared for the Secretary to follow.

Subba Row replied, denying putting on pressure. And he
wanted to see the guidelines! I was also keen to see them. I had
been told that they would marry up with my statement. I also
thought it was about time the Secretary and his colleagues were
defended by someone, other than David Clark, on the whole
question of whether the Committee had been aware of decisions
taken and their implementation. Of course, they had been. All
policy matters had been subject to the Committee's approval. I
asked the President to point this out to Subba Row, in

writing, so there could be no misunderstanding. He did so, finally.

It looked as if some sort of resolution was in sight, if not a wholly satisfactory one. I remained deeply concerned at the apparent unwillingness to follow the advice given by the Club's solicitor and counsel. I was particularly concerned at the avoidance of telling the members of MCC before irrevocable action was taken – whatever the outcome of that consultation. But now, at last, some important safeguards had been established by the Committee's acceptance of my paper.

Throughout the previous year, with all its arguments and conflicts, following Subba Row's all-out offensive I had been sorely tempted to cave in completely. 'Why not?' I often asked myself. 'Why not? There are only a few years to go and you can retire with honour as far as the MCC membership and the cricketing public are concerned. On the surface, MCC will be in all ways better off than when you became Secretary in 1974. You will have been one of the longer-serving Secretaries in the history of the Club and the record will show a job well done in difficult circumstances.

'Why should I not sell out? Why not simply coast along? Do as Colin Cowdrey, next year's President, plainly wants and fall in line with the demands made by the Chairman of TCCB. Hand over the jurisdiction of Lord's to the Test and County Cricket Board. Do as he suggests and paper over the difficulties, even if it may mean letting the staff sort out the resulting mess.

'The majority of the Committee are fighting shy of informing or consulting the membership about a fundamental change in the constitution. If only they would agree to do so, it would let you off the hook and give pause to the tactics being employed by Subba Row. Even if the results were unpalatable, at least the proper procedures would have been followed. The Club's solicitors and various counsel have advised a course of action which clearly points to consulting the members before rather than after the event. Even so, if a powerful section of the

Committee advocates differently, why should you worry? It is quite possible that the full implications will take a long time to surface. The truth will dawn, but so gradually as to be almost imperceptible. And it will be too late to concern you and your reputation. Forget the principles by which you have stood and which the Committee have, until recently, supported and, even now, many are loath to concede.

It may be some time before the Club is affected to any great degree. A change of TCCB Secretary is imminent. It is unlikely, for all sorts of reasons, that Alan Smith will prove as doggedly single-minded in pursuit of his own all-embracing objectives, or those of the TCCB hierarchy, as Donald Carr. The pass may have been sold by the time Smith takes over, but there is a fair chance that a great deal of damage limitation could be achieved. As a new boy at Lord's and with a reputation for discretion, A. C. Smith would certainly want to tread carefully.

'Forget the need to tell the membership. Forget that the Club will at times be at the mercy of a six-man TCCB Committee which has no elected part in the running of Lord's. Above all forget your personal pride and the position of the Secretary of MCC, whoever he may be, in future years; and the long-term diminution of the Club's standing in the world of cricket. Let the reins go and enjoy your cricketing friends. Live in the present, not the future, or indeed the past.'

I was aware that emotion as much as logic had governed my thoughts. But cricket, for all who know it well, is a passion, in many ways a reflection of life itself. What was the point of being Secretary of MCC if you weren't intimately involved in what went on at Lord's: past, present and future? There was little chance of escape from total involvement, even if you wanted it, when your whole working life was spent at the place, and you went home to a house behind the grandstand, and Father Time greeted you from your bedroom window each morning and you spent nearly twenty-four hours a day thinking, eating and drinking Lord's.

It made you possessive, proprietorial, proud, conscious of a great heritage. You became aware of responsibilities that could not be shirked and of the need to convince others of their importance. In a sense, you became the conscience of the Committee and that wasn't always kindly looked upon by those with their own axes to grind.

After nearly twelve years of resisting this bid for power without real responsibility, the MCC Committee had caved in on the basis that this was the better of two evils. The other evil being the threat (realistic or not) that major matches would be taken away from Lord's, if they did not toe the line.

It now seemed that I would have to live with certain adjustments. But at least the 'guidelines', yet to be prepared, would not go beyond the paper written by me and approved by the Committee, I thought.

Nonetheless, setting out in September 1986 for my first and only holiday of the year, I was left with a feeling of some uncertainty. Colin Cowdrey would take office in October.

The first meeting of the new MCC Committee, under Colin Cowdrey as President, was in the third week of that month. I wished that all business with the TCCB could have been concluded during Jack Davies's Presidency, as it should have been. It had always been intended that this be so, but the matter had dragged on interminably.

My thoughts turned, too often for my peace of mind, towards Cowdrey. He did not want a year as President which contained problems with the TCCB or anyone else. As someone with a sense of destiny and a large stake in the success of Michael Colin Cowdrey's year as President of MCC, his views would be short- rather than long-term. Small groups had been gathered round him before and after various dinners throughout the season, talking quietly. There were tales of a meeting with Subba Row at Wimbledon during the tennis championships in July. I had dined with him at his club; talked over with him in the Committee Room and in my office the whole problem of MCC's future relationship with the TCCB.

Yet I had gone as far as I could. The Committee knew me as

a man of my word. They knew I had done little wrong according to their policies. They had made it clear at their last meeting that my leaving was not an alternative to be considered. 'There are problems enough, don't look for more,' I told myself. 'You'll have enough difficulty keeping to whatever guidelines are produced. Unless they are the essence of clarity you will be on a hiding to nothing. Above all, the Committee will have to understand just exactly what commitment they are making on behalf of the Club.'

I returned from holiday in October to find that management of the Club's affairs had been virtually taken over by the new President and Sir Anthony Tuke. Talks had been held with TCCB about their advance cut from MCC's bicentenary match. Instead of the £120,000 which had been seen as the right sum to compensate for the loss of a match against Sri Lanka, these two had put forward £225,000. Had any mention been made of compensation to counties, or payment to clubs for the services of their players? Nobody had mentioned that. So a largish sum might have to be found over and above the £225,000. There was nothing to be done.

A meeting was held to consider the promised guidelines. It had been agreed that this would be done as a matter of course following their drafting by the other officers of the Club, apart from myself. Having seen them, I was full of misgivings. Perhaps I shouldn't have been, but I was. Couched overall in reasonable and sympathetic terms, they gave virtual *carte blanche* to TCCB, relied upon their goodwill not to use the freedom granted them indiscriminately, and while acknowledging that MCC had certain statutory obligations, said 'Generally speaking the Board (TCCB) should not use its powers to over-ride you on questions of security and crowd control, but the Committee cannot endorse a blanket exception of these areas from the TCCB's ultimate responsibility.'

I asked various friends on the Committee what I should best do in the circumstances. 'Try to get down to specifics,' was the consensus. 'Messrs Davies, Cowdrey and Tuke should know what they have in mind specifically.'

A meeting was held. I asked specific questions in relation to the guidelines. The varied answers I was given left me with no confidence that a common interpretation of the guidelines would be possible in the future.

The October meeting of the MCC Committee took place on the third Wednesday, as usual. As was customary, the President came to see the Secretary in the morning to discuss the agenda. Matters concerning TCCB were down as an item. It was agreed that this would be the first point; it was a big subject. The Committee had not seen the guidelines. We agreed that they would be gone through step by step and I would have the opportunity to ask for any points to be clarified, so that the Committee would be able at least to understand any reservations I might have and pronounce upon them.

There were as usual two meetings that afternoon. The first, of the General Purposes sub-committee, was marked by comments from the new President reflecting on the MCC Secretariat. The second – a meeting of the full MCC Committee – was about to begin when the President turned to me and said, 'Where can I find you?'

I was too dim to cotton on immediately. 'I shall be right here,' I replied.

'I want you and the rest of the Secretariat to leave,' he said.

'But our discussion this morning . . .' my voice trailed away.

I could see that he was determined to exclude me at all costs. The Secretariat were banished and took no part in the discussion on the guidelines.

Having spent twelve years as Secretary of MCC under distinguished Presidents from the varied worlds of banking, big business, politics, the diplomatic service and education, to name just a few, I thought I was equipped to deal with most things. But now a new dimension of behaviour had been introduced into my life. The President/Secretary relationship is a precious and delicate one, relying upon mutual confidence more than all else. There was clearly little point in my attempting to mend fences.

Having talked to David Clark and another member of the

Committee about what had happened in our absence, there seemed to be no real way forward. The Committee had discussed the guidelines when they were laid on the table, and apparently the impression had been given by the President not that I had sought clarification but that I had refused to accept the guidelines.

Cowdrey's next move was to present me with a written warning, drafted by lawyers, that I must accept the guidelines without further discussion and without reservation. The matter was obviously being dealt with outside Committee, and there was little I could do but resign. But when I talked to some lawyers who were expert in the field it was confirmed that resignation would leave me and mine exposed without any claims for the future. My letter to Cowdrey would have to be carefully phrased. I wrote in the following vein:

> I write to acknowledge your letter dated 5th November 1986 which I received yesterday on my return from India.
>
> I confirm that as instructed I will use my best endeavours to carry out the agreement entered into between the immediate past-President of MCC and the Chairman of TCCB as contained in their correspondence, and to work to the draft guidelines which you have assured me have been approved by the Committee.
>
> In coming to this decision, I have had very much at heart the interests of the Club and its members in their bicentennial year. I would, however, like assurance that at the end of the bicentennial year the whole position will be reviewed on a basis no less advantageous to my own position than the status quo prior to the meeting of the Committee held in October.
>
> I would trust it could be agreed that the formal warning issued by you will be withdrawn pending that review.

This proved unacceptable, as I feared it would. So after I had indicated my intention of resigning, it remained only for a final agreement to be drawn up and signed by both parties before I went to Australia at the kind invitation of the Australian Cricket Board in December.

I went out with Raman Subba Row and J.J. Warr. Warr was a member of the MCC Committee but was travelling to Australia partly as an Australian representative on ICC, partly on business. Despite the anguish of the last months it was a reasonably convivial time, and everyone in Australia was so friendly, and the Australian Board members so welcoming, that I could hardly bear the thought that this would be my last visit to Australia as Secretary of MCC.

I had understood that any statement to the press about my resignation would be the subject of agreement between the MCC Committee and myself. But, perhaps because of a misunderstanding between Cowdrey and me, one was released while I was still in Australia.

11

THE STORM BREAKS

THE COMMITTEE'S STATEMENT to the press was pretty muted and was not picked up by Fleet Street as anything remarkable: the early retirement of the MCC Secretary was not, after all, a story of great consequence for the general reader. However, Richard Streeton of *The Times* was astute enough to ring the Treasurer, David Clark, only to learn that he had also resigned. Streeton pieced together a responsible and well written story. By then it had become apparent that the agreement I had made with Colin Cowdrey and Sir Anthony Tuke about public utterances on the subject of my going had been dented, if not shattered, by some of the stuff appearing in the press. One article, at least, indicated that Cowdrey had been consulted. The understanding I had reached which stipulated that neither side would go beyond a simple press statement issued by the MCC Committee, had clearly put me at a disadvantage in keeping to my end of the bargain.

I did not retire officially until the end of January 1987, and spent a few days negotiating the final agreement. The terms were reasonable by most standards but not as generous as David Clark thought they should have been after what he called twenty years wholehearted service to cricket and to MCC. It was easy to see that David Clark could have been biased in my favour. He had been Treasurer of MCC for six years or so, and President in 1976 and 1977, and we had grown to respect each other enormously, even if we had not always seen eye to eye on every single thing. I rated him highly as a man of integrity.

During my last days I spent a lot of time answering a great many kind and sympathetic letters from friends in the cricket world and members of the Club including a large number from fellow administrators and others overseas. And together with Michael Sissons of the MCC Committee, I pursued various negotiations with BBC TV and radio in regard to MCC's forthcoming bicentenary match.

I moved out of my office at Lord's with a full heart. One of the many phone calls I received during the ensuing weeks was from an erstwhile colleague of my rugby football writing days. John Reason, chief rugby correspondent of the *Sunday Telegraph*, was also an MCC member and a journalist with a nose for a story. He also knew me; had done so for a long time. He could not, he said, wholly believe what had been appearing in the cricket press. Would I like to give my side of the story? I explained that it was impossible for me to do so. Under the terms of my severance I could not make statements to the media. I suggested he might wish to talk to David Clark who had resigned as Treasurer and was under no such obligation. Reason must have been very busy. On 26 April he reported on the (unconfirmed by them) disquiet of MCC's solicitors at the contents of a letter sent by Colin Cowdrey, President of MCC, to the members. He also reported on the further disquiet of MCC's solicitors at the contents of the Annual Report.

'The report,' he wrote, 'virtually ignored the traumatic build-up to the departure of Bailey and Clark in the bicentenary year and also plays down the ungenerous letter sent to members by Colin Cowdrey . . .

'In that letter Bailey was portrayed as the "baddie" who was preventing the Test and County Cricket Board from doing what they liked at Lord's despite the fact that Bailey was employed by MCC and not by TCCB and despite the fact that Lord's cricket ground is owned by MCC.

'No evidence was produced to show what Bailey had done wrong or whether he had acted against the interests of MCC or against the instructions of the MCC Committee.

'The fact that Clark resigned on principle in support of Bailey was also ignored in the report.'

The article pointed to the near-impossible position in which the Club's lawyers were placed, pointed to the Club rules and the apparent skirting of them with regard to the 'over-seventy' rule. He referred to the severe problems faced by George Mann and Doug Insole in the context of divided loyalties and the problems faced by MCC as a result.

On 3 May 1987, the Sunday prior to the following Wednesday's MCC Annual General Meeting, John Reason really went to town. In trenchant terms he explored the themes which had led to the departure of David Clark and myself and had caused the Club's solicitor to withdraw support for the Annual Report presented to the Club's members.

The Club's solicitors were in a very awkward position. They knew the affairs of the Club inside out. They had been responsible for giving advice on all manner of topics, had acted for the Club for decades. The Club Rules, the Rules of ICC had all come within their domain, as had the Packer and London Weekend Television court hearings.

Now they had sought the advice of leading counsel regarding the whole TCCB/MCC matter, advice which they had passed on to the Committee, had sought advice on the Working Party report which had likewise been conveyed. Now they were in no man's land. Having given and sought opinions on the proper procedure for the Annual General Meeting, they found that matters had gone beyond a point where, in all conscience, they could support the Committee in the line it was taking. It was courageous on their part to stand by their guns and in the end they were to pay dearly for it.

John Reason went on to mention the years of steadily increasing pressure from the TCCB Executive Committee, their bid to increase both their authority over matches played at Lord's and over their already considerable share of the member's facilities there. He pointed to the financial conditions forced upon MCC by TCCB and the losses to MCC membership as a result. He highlighted the abandonment of the working party report following its acceptance by the Committee and by the membership without telling the members, the legal advice that the Committee should go to the members before accepting TCCB's demands, and the Committee's failure to do so.

Before and after the Annual General Meeting (which I did not attend) I entertained a number of friends at my house. *The Times* correspondent remarked how sad it was that so many of the dissidents used the Secretary's (my) home as a base; as though some enemy camp had been set up in Elm Tree Road. I had known most of my guests for ages – all of them, except David Clark and two recent members of the MCC Committee, Fred Millett and Colin Smith, ordinary members of the Club. All called to express their condolences, genuinely concerned, as friends are liable to be, over the turn affairs had taken. One of those present, a friend of a friend, was unknown to me before that day. He was Nigel Knott. He had read John Reason's article, and was concerned that the truth should come out. He flourished a copy of the working party report.

'How do I get the President to answer various questions I want to put?' he asked me.

'It's very difficult,' I acknowledged. 'But I believe that the Chairman would be hard put not to ask you to speak if you raised a point of order.'

That was the extent of our conversation on the subject of the Annual General Meeting, the extent of the 'gathering of dissidents' mentioned by *The Times* man. The outcome of that AGM is well known: for the first time in the Club's history the Report and Accounts were not adopted. A member, Robin Bourne, also unknown to me at the time, summed up the meeting in a letter to the press which contained the following passages:

'The vote ... was overwhelming. So much so, the President, incredulous and confused, put the motion to adopt a second time. The result of this ill-advised move was, if anything, even more overwhelming.

'In view of the reported remarks of the Club Secretary that it was not a vote of no confidence, it is only fair to members who were not able to be present to inform them that the vote came as close to being one of no confidence as was possible without making such a motion specifically.

'The fact is that the meeting was chaotic from start to finish and was a demonstration of the Committee's incompetence. Accommodation was totally inadequate. . . . A large number of members couldn't get in and it was fortunate the vote was clear cut.

'. . . Even now we are not clearly informed of the safeguards that are supposed to have been agreed with TCCB for members' rights and privileges.

'However it did become clear that Jack Bailey had consistently stood for the interests of MCC members and that gradually the Committee was conceding more and more to the demands of the TCCB. There was no doubt that the members were right behind him on that.'

The letter went on to criticize the fact that TCCB had been guaranteed £225,000 from the proceeds of the MCC's bi-centenary match and that they could only hold the fixture on their own ground with the consent of TCCB. And continued:

'. . . the way forward is for the (Annual) Report to be amended so that the Club's lawyers can endorse it and for the AGM to be reconvened. Yesterday it was adjourned before the business of the meeting was completed. There should be no question of trying to push through the Report as it stands by the device of a postal vote.

'... Running the Club behind closed doors with little reference to the membership should come to an end. That was what yesterday's meeting was about.'

The Times correspondent was and is a great friend of Colin Cowdrey and a considerable friend of mine. Like so many commentators, within the game though detached from it, he could see the wood for the trees, but were they the right wood and the right trees?

'To take the heat out of Wednesday's meeting,' he wrote, 'all that was needed could have been a clear statement of the terms of TCCB's rights (they have been much the same for the last eight years) together with reassurances that MCC's patrimony was being forcefully and strictly protected and would never be further compromised without being put to the vote.'

But was that really the case?

For one thing the MCC Committee had clearly been forced to give TCCB, as a result of the previous twelve months, rights far beyond anything previously contemplated. For another, MCC's 'patrimony' was *not* being forcefully and strictly protected. The main hope was that it might be now that the members were aware of what had been going on.

How would it have sounded to the members at the Annual General Meeting if a clear statement had been made along the following lines?

The TCCB constitution in respect of cricket matches has not changed materially since 1968, but as a result of continuous pressure exerted on the Committee and the Secretariat, which rose to a crescendo during 1986, and despite legal opinions to the contrary, the rights granted to TCCB at Lord's include the following:

1. The overall and ultimate responsibility and authority for staging first-class matches at Lord's. In general terms this

means that the will of TCCB and its servants shall prevail in all matters and this will apply at Lord's before and during the cricket matches in question.

2. The Secretary and consequently the Secretariat and staff of MCC will be subject to the direction of TCCB representatives. The MCC Committee have waived their responsibilities in this respect, although they are solely responsible for the management of the Club under the Rules of MCC and as set out in the working party report approved by the Committee and adopted by the members of MCC in May 1984, and still not rescinded by them.

3. The Committee agreed to these terms and conditions in the expectation that they would receive some form of guarantee from TCCB as to the continuation of the staging of major matches at Lord's. No such undertaking has been forthcoming.

4. The MCC Committee has made it clear to the TCCB that if the TCCB should exercise their authority in such a way as to *seriously* affect members' rights, the Committee would be bound to put the matter to the membership before taking action.

5. TCCB have made it clear to MCC that the rights of MCC members are just the same as those of county members on other grounds. If the TCCB seeks to limit those rights it should enter into discussion with MCC regarding that requirement. It should be borne in mind that the provisions of paragraph 1 will apply as an over-riding factor.

If such a statement had been made it would have been nearer to the true position. But would it have gone down well?

It gave me no pleasure to see MCC in such turmoil. There is nothing worse in life than civil war, when friend turns against friend, and friendship and even respect are forgotten in the need to defend one's own position. Now the MCC Committee were forced to man the ramparts and defend them with every means at their disposal. There was, of course, nothing I could say or do in defence of myself or anyone else.

Meanwhile, Alan Meyer, MCC's solicitor, was in an awkward spot indeed. Before the Annual General Meeting, he had written to the President and the new Secretary; had had meetings with the President and others, in an attempt to explain why he could not support them in what they had seen fit to disclose to the members. At the AGM he had been placed in the unenviable position of making it clear to the membership that there were various aspects of the Annual Report and Cowdrey's letter to the members which he found untenable. As the Club's legal adviser for more than twenty years on a personal basis, with a responsibility to the membership, but employed by the Committee, his path was studded with pitfalls. Now he was faced with offering advice as to how best the damage might be limited. He had always been in favour of full and frank disclosure, but could the Committee afford such a course? Above all, could certain individuals at the centre of power be persuaded that they had not acted properly?

The facts were that the Annual General Meeting had been halted by the President when a great deal of important business remained unfinished. Part of that business was connected with a proposal of F. W. Millett and A. J. G. Waters which, in effect, asked for certain assurances about the future running of the Club and a full discussion of the pros and cons. It was never concluded. Even the nomination of the Club's next President was made outside the meeting, contrary to the Rules.

It was a nice point whether, as the Report and Accounts had been thrown out, anything passed at the meeting relating to that Report and those Accounts was valid. It seemed certain that morally, if not legally, the AGM should be called again, the Committee should put all their cards on the table in a document to members beforehand, and ask for the Report and Accounts to be passed on the basis of full information.

The Committee took a tough, pragmatic line. They dispensed with the services of MCC's solicitors whose firm had been involved with MCC for sixty years, and employed instead a large partnership. They called a Special General Meeting to consider anew the Report and Accounts (at least those parts of the Report and Accounts they considered it appropriate to discuss) and they prepared a document noteworthy for its length and for the selectivity of the enlightenment it provided.

Meanwhile, a group of members had formed themselves into an action group. Nigel Knott, the man who had asked embarrassing questions at the Annual General Meeting, Alick Waters, an administrator par excellence, and a number of others, sought and paid for independent legal advice.

They asked for a transcript of the Annual General Meeting, if it had been recorded. Yes, the meeting had been recorded and transcribed but the transcript was not available to ordinary members on grounds of confidentiality and cost. Knott, Waters and company offered to pay any cost, but to no avail.

They collected 240 signatures of members of MCC, more than enough to call a Special General Meeting under the rules, only to find the Committee had called their own and would not allow those members who dissented from the Committee line to put any point of view in the mailing that went out to members. An offer by Knott and company to share the costs of the mailing was refused.

Nigel Knott and the solicitor employed by a growing band of warriors, who felt the members should know the whole truth about the past year, were invited to Lord's, after much badgering on their part, to meet the President, Colin Cowdrey, and the Treasurer, Hubert Doggart – in loco parentis until after the Special Meeting – and John Stephenson, my successor as Secretary. They were wined and dined but were not impressed.

All requests were, naturally enough, referred to the Committee, who finally agreed to discuss the form of the Special General Meeting to be held on 30 July but made no further concessions to Knott or the 240 signatories who had asked for full disclosure.

The signatories were on a hiding to nothing. The document circulated by the Committee with no other contrary information or point of view was accepted by an overwhelming majority of those who voted. In the hall, at the Special Meeting itself, the result was much the same. It was bound to be. No matter how right they might have been, sheer organizational and financial strength were always in the Committee's favour.

It was also right that the Committee won the day, for the Club's continued well-being, even if the policies had been controversial, was of supreme importance. If only the members had been consulted in the first place, before the events of 1986 and early 1987, a great deal of angst would have been avoided and a lot less blood would have been spilled, and far fewer friends would have been at each other's throats.

12

AND FOR MY NEXT TRICK . . .

SINCE I WALKED out of Lord's for the last time as Secretary
of MCC and of ICC, a number of improvements to the
ground have come to a conclusion. The new Mound stand has
been completed, and very handsome it looks. The new elec-
tronic scoreboard is in place. Bucket seats, given impetus by the
strict regulations arising out of the Bradford stadium fire disaster, are rapidly gobbling up those lovely old benches, and
other steps towards making the place a 'blue chip' stadium are
doubtless on the drawing board or beyond. More advertising
revenue, but no room for the ordinary fellow to sit on benches
near the boundary, or on the grass, was a forseeable change. It
was a step which has made crowds at big matches easier to
handle and has also been the means of allaying the considerable
losses to the MCC's revenue, brought about by the new means
of distribution decreed by TCCB. Quite simply, advertising
sites are more profitable than people.

But I live in hope that the essential qualities of Lord's, beyond
all other Test match grounds, are preserved. The ability to walk

all round the ground and, with the exception of a brief interlude when passing behind the Mound stand, to gain a view of the cricket, is to retain that intimacy between crowd and players, that village atmosphere which I believe is an integral part of the character of the place. Whether it can be achieved or not, I don't know.

The pavilion, if further improved, will, I hope, always retain its unique atmosphere, the very smell of antiquity. First as a cricketer, and then as an administrator who spent the greater part of his life in the pavilion, I could never quite pin down the sobering, even awesome effect of walking through the Long Room. It is a feeling very few who have made the trip, through the Long Room and down those steps to the middle, will gainsay, or will be able accurately to describe. Quite apart from the impressive oil paintings of cricketing giants from the past, or the beautifully ornate ceiling or those wonderful old stools and long tables on which the members sit, or the great windows looking out onto the field, there is an indefinable something beyond the sum of all those parts which hits you, be the great room full or empty. After years of thought, I have never been able quite to pin it down. The nearest I have been able to get to qualifying the mysterious ingredient is to put it down to the cleaning fluid and the soap and water and the polish with which the floors and tables were cleaned every day of the working week. Could it be that those tasks performed by Tony Archdale or Harry the Hat (so called because, outdoors or in, he was never seen without his fedora planted firmly on his head) supplied the missing ingredient? Certainly it was a different world you entered when passing through the swing doors to another part of the pavilion.

The Committee Room, which often produced a form of nervous tension whenever I entered it, has been the scene of much pondering over recent times. It seems that the financiers have been hard at work. Members have seen the subscription rise in 1989 by about 40 per cent. The marketing men have moved in too. Entertaining has long been a feature at Lord's but now the numerous boxes are let to corporations, no longer exclusively to members. The Keith Prowse marquees, the hot-dog and hamburger facilities in the once serene Coronation Gardens just behind the pavilion, are sure signs of a not-too-subtle change of emphasis, just as the huge advertisement for Foster's Lager hits you as you enter through the Grace Gates. Foster's Lord's? No, it is actually The Oval which will in future integrate its name with the amber nectar. One lives in real hope that we will not get to the stage of (say) Ladbroke's Lord's or Tesco's Trent Bridge, but then everything seems to have its price. And MCC are still in debt to the tune of some £2 million as a result of financing part of the building of the new Mound stand on the basis of interest-free loans instead of by more orthodox borrowing methods.

The production of the Annual Report to members along the lines of a glossy company report to shareholders is another innovation, and the members are now being written to fairly regularly by incoming Presidents. McKinsey have been in to examine the workings of the administration and have taken their money and gone.

There will be those who, reasonably enough, gain encouragement from these happenings: keeping up with the times and all that. However, it is also important that the Committee and the membership in general do not stray from the basic traditions which have sustained the Club, just as they have sustained cricket, over the years.

Although turning to journalism as a way of turning the odd penny since leaving Lord's, I have generally been careful not to rush into print about matters concerning the great Club, even though there have been things done which I might have wished had been done differently, or not at all. One issue did, however, cause me to put pen to paper. It was the subject of considerable correspondence in *The Times*, before I wrote, and I wrote only because Hubert Doggart, the MCC Treasurer, had written along lines seeking to justify a position which the Committee had taken and which I, and clearly a number of others, felt was untenable. The article I wrote is reprinted here:

I refer to the letter recently received by those on the waiting list for membership and to which the recipient is expected to reply by September 1st, enclosing a cheque for £50. What has happened is an embarrassment, not only for the candidate, but for the member who proposed or seconded him.

At the time of his proposal the candidate could have been made aware that there was an inordinately long waiting-list for membership. According to custom, he would have been entered on that list with the knowledge that his turn would come in the fullness of time and then, and only then, would his suitability for election be assessed by the MCC Committee. Apart from those who qualified as cricketers good enough to represent the Club, nobody would be allowed to vault over him. His place in the queue was secure.

The same candidate has now been informed that the rules have changed. In order to retain the place, he will have to stump up £50. True, when the time comes (assume, for the sake of argument, that this will be in 1998), this £50 will be deducted from his entrance fee, always provided that he is elected.

By then his £50, even if most conservatively invested, will be worth at least £100 to the Club, but not to him. What is more, the poor fellow, having gone through the proper electoral procedures in 1998, could well be turned down for whatever good reason, but his £50 (now £100) will, according to the letter received, in no circumstances be refunded.

Retrospective action such as is now proposed, which affects not the present membership, who would have some means of redress, but those without any say in the Club's affairs, is doubly dangerous. On the one hand lies the alienation of those men of principle who may not be short of the odd £50 but who strongly object to the rules being changed when the match has already started. These are the very people MCC needs as members, who will serve the Club loyally in the future.

On the other hand there is an indefinable feeling that MCC, of all the clubs in the world, is fostering something which is not cricket. Nor is it right that the man who says he will pay up happily in order to claw his way up the list should benefit in that way. The power of the pound is strong but it should not influence the position of those aspiring to membership of MCC.

By all means seek confirmation that in all the present circumstances the candidate wishes to remain on the list. At the same time make it clear to all new candidates what the likely waiting time will be.

Ask all new candidates for a registration fee for £50 as an earnest of their intent. Since £50 is half the 1989 entrance fee, make it clear that this payment will count as 50 per cent of the entrance fee in force when he is elected, thus ensuring that its value is maintained.

Is it too late for the MCC Committee to think again? It is reported that it meets this week. The Lord's Test match starts on Thursday. There is surely time for the matter to be reviewed. For the sake of MCC and its future, I hope it will be.

There have been, so I understand, some second thoughts. At least the man on the waiting-list who does not get selected will receive repayment of his enforced donation. But my main fear is that those potential members of character whom the Club badly needs, may now have left the waiting-list because they object in principle to the moving of goalposts in an arbitrary and retrospective way.

On the international front, signs are not at all encouraging. The banning of certain England players, selected to go to India in 1988 in accord with ICC rules which had been enforced by ICC resolutions, was a body blow to the ICC and the future of international cricket.

An additional twist was given to the Indian action. On this occasion, the cricket authorities came out in full support of their government's action, and did so publicly. This departure from precedent can only mean that the Indian Cricket Board opted out of the obligations of ICC membership. On the one hand they were party to an agreement among cricketing nations. On the other hand, they were seen to be endorsing steps which led to the cancellation of a tour already agreed between them and England under conditions which had not been contravened.

The cricket world was left to contemplate the results of having a distinguished Indian politician at the centre of their Board's decision-making process.

Nothing should really surprise us. But the cynicism of the decision made in 1988, when compared with the treatment of those same players when they were allowed to participate in the admirably staged World Cup, less than a year previously, had little to do with cricket. Of course, the banning of anyone from participation in the World Cup would have led to grievous losses of money and prestige. The banning of England players for a scheduled tour of India was far less damaging in those terms.

In fact it was English cricket that was now faced with a considerable financial loss, as a result of India's action. The chosen players were being paid, with no compensating income from the Indian tour. The fact that it was the English authorities who cancelled, finally, augured badly for any claim for recompense.

Troubles with India had followed hard on the heels of events in Pakistan during the English winter of 1987–88; England's disastrous summer against the touring West Indians; and the second and third volumes of the Mike Gatting saga. All those matters fell within the province (in the absence of any apparent role for the game's nominal governing body, the Cricket Council) of the TCCB.

Perhaps there is now too much power in too few hands. Perhaps the apparent system of delegation, the management structure, has developed along the wrong lines. Perhaps a bit of both. Certainly the events of the 1987–88 winter and the English summer of 1988 have seen a few chickens come home to roost.

I can safely deny suggestions, sometimes made to me, that I must have had many a smile at the way things have turned out. For one thing, for anyone with the game at heart, matters have been too serious to warrant many smiles, however wry. There is no satisfaction to be gained from watching cricket lose its way. If events have confirmed rather than alleviated my mistrust of the system currently operating in the English game, there is no great cause for rejoicing on that score. Far from it. Yet I have been surprised how those at the centre of power within TCCB appear to have been caught so often with their trousers down. They have the game at heart. They are genuine and sincere men. All have served cricket, or various aspects of it, for a considerable time, in various contexts.

The circumstances surrounding the 1987–88 tour of Pakistan by England had one friend of mine likening the attempts by TCCB to sort out the Gatting/Umpire Rana fracas to a drunk staggering from lamp post to lamp post. Certainly, there did seem to be a bewildering series of statements and counter-statements issuing from Lord's, guaranteed to throw the man in the street into confusion. First, the whole matter was one for the management in Pakistan, the officials on the spot, to sort out. On the face of it that was the only solution worth pursuing. There can be little doubt, however, that the Pakistan Board and its chosen delegates were in no mind to be helpful to those on the spot. Whenever the differing views of either side on the justice or injustice of a particular set of circumstances is conducted in a series of inspired leaks through the press, the situation is ready-made for disaster. Another inherent problem lay in the appointment of managerial personnel on a three-year contractual basis as paid employees. Over-identification with the players with their own narrower view of the game is an almost inevitable consequence, just as that identification is a handicap when seen through the eyes of the opposition. The Pakistan fiasco should have been resolved, on the spot; but could it have been, given the obvious distrust of both parties in the intentions of the other?

The answer is probably that it could have been if there had been an insistence upon the Rules of the ICC, which govern the appointment of umpires during Test matches, being followed. A procedure is laid down whereby objections by the visiting teams to a certain umpire can and generally should be met. If Mike Gatting's own account of events is accurate, these rules were not followed by the Pakistan authorities from Day One of that ill-fated tour. The England management could surely have insisted that they were. Matters would have been brought to a head much earlier; and the pressures brought upon the Pakistan authorities to resolve any differences properly and satisfactorily would have come before the Test matches were played, and before any further fuel could be added to the already combustible relations between the TCCB and the Pakistan Board. These had smouldered since 1982 and were fanned in 1987 in England when TCCB refused to acknowledge positively Pakistan's objections to Umpire Constant, which they had also done in 1982.

Going on from there, the volatile Chris Broad's unwillingness to leave the wicket when given out, and the subsequent lack of demonstrably effective action, saw England surrender the high moral ground which has generally, though not always, been theirs when touring abroad. Once the basic code of behaviour had been seriously undermined by both sides, and once the atmosphere had become impossible with the England captain and a Pakistan umpire at visible and continuous odds on the field of play, the whole sorry affair was bound to end in tears. The subsequent order to Gatting to apologize, so as to get the game started at all costs, and the visit to Pakistan by Raman Subba Row, the Chairman, and Alan Smith the Secretary were probably inevitable, once the Foreign Office had been consulted about the situation in a highly sensitive country. But the award of a £1000 bonus to each member of the England touring party by the Chairman of TCCB, apparently off his own bat? That is one gesture I shall never understand and one which has left even players and administrators of my acquaintance thoroughly bemused.

Since then an Australian touring party has taken issue with Pakistan over the standard of their umpiring. It has been implied, if not stated, that cheating was the order of the day during the first Test match between the two countries in 1988. Ironically, in view of Australia's own understandable but sometimes questionable attitude to ICC interference in such matters, a call has been made for the International Cricket Conference to look into the whole question of umpiring in Pakistan. In the early 1980s the Pakistan Board had asked for unaligned umpires to be appointed for all Test matches.

These conflicts, and those arising internally in England during the 1988 season in this country, are symptomatic of a game which needs to re-assess its priorities. And there have been casualties: the morale of England's Test team for one, that likeable man, Mike Gatting for another – and the credibility of the England selectors for a third.

Without going into the whys and wherefores of the 'revelations' in the *Sun* which apparently cost Gatting the captaincy, there must be questions about the way the whole thing was handled.

Why was the responsibility for assessing the suitability of Gatting to captain England on grounds outside his abilities on the field apparently left to the selectors to deal with? Surely some other committee, connected with discipline, or the TCCB itself should have taken that responsibility? Surely the highest authority should have been responsible for making it clear to the public how and for what reason or reasons such a drastic step had been taken? Why were other England players, mentioned in the same tawdry article as having misbehaved themselves in a Leicestershire hotel, summoned to Lord's in such a public manner, to be quizzed about their behaviour? By short-cutting proper procedures and by doing so publicly, the TCCB itself lost marks and innocent players who were hauled up before the selectors were thoroughly disgruntled; and with good cause.

There could be no more pleasant or conscientious man than Mickey Stewart. He did an excellent job on his first tour, as assistant manager on the cricket side. But what was he doing as England's manager in England? Why, suddenly, were the traditional roles of captain and chairman of selectors altered to no great purpose except to confuse? A coach, yes. A manager, no.

In 1988, England had a chairman of selectors who came increasingly under fire, a manager whose job may be well defined but is not easily discerned, and five captains in all — none of whom was able to establish himself in the traditional role for one reason or another, and at least two of whom clearly considered themselves as having been poorly treated.

Before his troubles in Pakistan, Gatting had been good at getting his team around him, was an outstanding player — which held their respect — and was tactically sound. Having been appointed following that tour, his involvement with the opposite sex was said on behalf of the selectors to have been relatively innocent, yet he was relieved of his post, with no obvious successor having been groomed. The grounds were, presumably, that whatever he did or did not do, it was the straw that broke the camel's back. The subsequent publication of his book broke his contractual obligations, so that, at least in retrospect, the decision to bring in a new captain had been justified.

The appointed captain should never be relieved of his total responsibility for the conduct of his team and of himself both on and off the field. The chairman of selectors has an awesome task in assisting the captain in every possibly way, not least by giving him the best possible team. Get the right captain and the right chairman and you don't need a manager in England. In 1988 it seemed that all three were on a hiding to nothing.

The manager abroad must know his cricket and his cricketers. But he cannot be put in a position where it becomes impossible to take a step back from his team and view the best interests of the game at large. For this reason an assistant manager to a touring team can be a great asset, but he should not be the only member of the management team with knowledge of the game from the inside. The manager, the assistant manager and the captain should have no doubts that their main duties are to the game as a whole, before all else. Otherwise cricket is lost, whoever wins the contest. The problem of over-identification with the team and its naturally insular outlook is of course made more difficult by the appointment of a manager for a period of more than one tour at a time. Continuity in this case can be a bad thing. The chance of review should always be there.

All of which shows how difficult a game cricket is to administer. The rule of thumb, though, even in a changing world, must be to stick to tried and trusted principles right from the beginning of any venture.

Cricket will, I hope, cling, however tenuously, to the ethics which made it such a great game. The voice of Marylebone Cricket Club has become so muted, their influence even at Lord's being on the wane, that it is difficult to see how the best things for which they have always stood will avoid being submerged, as other priorities take over.

A great many of the peculiarities surrounding English cricket come as a result of its being out of step with other Test match playing countries in terms of its domestic scene. England's defeats at the hands of the West Indies have been variously blamed on the presence of too many overseas players in the county game; too much one-day cricket; three-day cricket instead of four-day cricket; and the dearth of good batting wickets on the Test and county scene. Well, there may be something in all that. But the need to support a fully professional game since the early 1960s, when it was dying through lack of appeal and financial support, brought into being those very factors which are now being decried as damaging to England's chances. Perhaps some readjustment is necessary, but while England's professional game continues (and long may it do so) the need to entertain, as well as to win, will always be there. When you come right down to it, England were beaten in 1988 by a team of better players, made potent by a battery of fast bowling from which there was no respite and a captain who spared no effort to gather his side around him and worked hard throughout the tour to get the best out of them.

The future may, after all, lie more in a limitation on dangerous fast short-pitched bowling, a decisive factor in too many Tests for far too long, than in any other single facet of the game, and that is a matter for the International Cricket Conference.

The South African saga may appear on the surface to have been ended by decisions taken at the ICC meeting in January 1989. Prospective bans from international cricket for a limited number of years on players plying their trade in South Africa, whether as coaches or players, is almost certainly a decision which would meet the requirements of the English courts. In the light of the judgement in the Packer case (doubtless one of the matters considered carefully by their former adversary, Lord Alexander of Weedon, when tendering advice to the cricket authorities in England) unfair restraint of trade would be difficult to show. Nor does incitement to breach a lawful contract seem a likely issue in view of the prospective nature of the bans.

It was virtually inevitable that such a limited ban should be sanctioned first by the TCCB, in spite of a natural reluctance on the part of some countries to prevent individuals earning a perfectly legal and honest living. It was made inevitable by the wide publication in the national media of a supposedly confidential document, addressed to county chairmen, setting out the pros and cons of such action, long before a meeting was held to consider the question. This pre-empting of a calm assessment and unsullied discussion by a sort of press trial based on a number of selected considerations was an interesting development. It would appear to ensure that TCCB decisions of importance will actually rest in the hands of the executive, given that similar public relations exercises have been carried out before those theoretically responsible for a decision sit down to meet.

A similar exercise was set in train before discussions about the next England chairman of selectors. No appointment had been made, no consideration given by the full TCCB before the hype began and the counties were put under considerable pressure to approve their executive committee's recommendation.

In such a climate as prevailed during consideration of the South African question, anyone advocating such out-moded principles as the right of individuals who are cricketers to earn a lawful living as they feel inclined, in the same way as people in other walks of life, would receive short shrift.

Whether they would have been right or wrong is not the issue, anymore than the outcome of the ICC meeting is at issue. There was clearly a case to be made for expediency, pragmatism – call it what you will. The need to stand by the South African cricket authorities and individual cricketers had to be weighed against the need to put Test match cricket between member countries on a more certain footing.

Whether the ICC decision will achieve this is by no means certain. What can be accepted is that the proposal that cricketers going th South Africa should be subject to a life ban, which for some strange reason remained on the January agenda of the ICC, would never be a starter in a English court of law. Perhaps leaving it intact enabled what was done to appear to be a satisfactory compromise.

The fact is, though, that the ICC have now taken part of the problem away from politicians and saddled themselves with it. Nor does any ban by ICC prevent any government, from Guyana to New Zealand, from refusing entry to England cricketers with South African connections, even if they do fulfil the requirements of the ICC decision. Round the corner lurk still Sam Ramsamy, SACOS, the United Nations' anti-apartheid committee with their black list, and individual politicians in many countries.

Conflicts in cricket are far from being at an end. As Al Jolson was wont to say, 'You ain't heard nothing yet.'

However, it is no longer my responsibility to influence or to guide. My own role in cricket is at best peripheral in the decision-making sense. All I can do, as a commentator on the game for *The Times*, is to enjoy my continued involvement, go on realizing that it is easier on the outside than when you are involved in the heat of the kitchen, and to make as certain as I can that a sense of enthusiasm is conveyed for one of the most friendly and complicated and skilful of pursuits known to man. It is a considerable challenge and I am very glad to have been given it.